Hopeful
IMAGINATIN

Traditional Churches Finding God's Way
in a Changing World

MIKE QUEEN & JAYNE DAVIS

*Cooperative Baptist Fellowship of North Carolina (http://cbfnc.org)
has sponsored the publication of this book.*

© 2014

Published in the United States by Nurturing Faith Inc., Macon GA,
www.nurturingfaith.net.

Library of Congress Cataloging-in-Publication Data is available.

ISBN 978-1-938514-52-4

Contents

*To the amazing congregation and staff of First Baptist Church,
Wilmington, North Carolina, and to our wonderful families
who have supported us in our ministries.*

Foreword

Christian congregations, like just about everything else in our culture, are undergoing tremendous change. That's not a huge revelation. Almost everyone involved with congregations agrees with that statement, because we live with that reality.

One of the central changes for congregations today is that they are no longer the center of social and cultural life in most communities. Today, depending on where you live, churches are somewhere between slightly off center and all the way at the margins of centers of social influence in their communities. Perhaps no group of churches has experienced this shift more dramatically than "Old First" churches.

Another change is that denominational organizations are no longer the repository of all resources, services, and expertise that congregations need to be effective. Often, the true "experts" are not denominational organizations, but other congregations. The best denominational organizations see their task, primarily, as cultivating a network of churches and ministry partners and connecting them to one another as a community of mutual learning and resourcing.

With these changes in mind, Cooperative Baptist Fellowship of North Carolina (CBFNC) partnered with First Baptist Church Wilmington and others in 2010 to produce the first "Hopeful Imagination" conference. The centerpiece of the conference was telling the story of FBC Wilmington in the words of its leaders. It was a story of how an "Old First" church adapted to our changing times and managed not only to survive, but also to thrive.

In addition to the resource of the FBC story, we brought in other leaders who made contributions to the corporate learning. Teams of congregational leaders attended the conference, listened to the stories, and returned home to apply their learning in their own congregations and communities.

Ministers Mike Queen and Jayne Davis have now compiled some of this information in book form as a way for you to experience the benefit of that conference. It's a way for a much larger group of congregational leadership colleagues to share their learning with one another as we seek to be faithful to God's call to be transformed and transformative in the changing times in which we all find ourselves.

We have no better leaders to take us on this journey than Mike and Jayne. Not only can they take us back to experience and understand the twenty-five-year transformational sojourn of FBC Wilmington, but also more importantly, they can help each of us and our congregations to take a similar—though never identical—journey of faithfulness in the pursuit of God's mission. Mike and Jayne are gifted communicators and effective leaders. They are joyful conversation partners. And to me and a growing number of colleagues, they are wonderful friends.

My strong advice to pastors and congregational leaders is this:

• Pull together a group of leaders from your church who are spiritually and emotionally healthy and who are respected by fellow church members, but who are not content with maintaining the status quo.
• Secure a copy of this book for each person in the group.
• Gather once every week or two to study a chapter of this book together.
• Listen to Mike and Jayne and the Holy Spirit as they tell the First Baptist Wilmington story.
• Explore how the FBC Wilmington story intersects with your congregation's story.
• Let Jayne guide you by completing the exercises she suggests.
• Dream together of what God may be leading your congregation to be and do in ways that are inspired by, but never a duplication of, the remarkable example of FBC Wilmington.
• Allow these friends to help you cultivate a "hopeful imagination" for the future of your church.

After Mike's retirement from the pastorate of FBC Wilmington, he told me that he and Jayne were planning to start a ministry with the same title as the 2010 conference. Their goal, he said, was to help old churches and young ministers. I believe their ministry, beginning with this book, will find a much larger audience.

Larry Hovis
Executive Coordinator
CBF of North Carolina

The Best Is Yet to Be

*Practicing Hopeful Imagination is to believe
that our best days are still ahead of us.*

"Moses was keeping the flock of his father-in-law Jethro, the priest of Midian; he led his flock beyond the wilderness, and came to Horeb, the mountain of God. There the angel of the Lord appeared to him in a flame of fire out of a bush; he looked, and the bush was blazing, yet it was not consumed" (Exod. 3:1-2 NRSV).

You know this story well. In that holy moment, Moses was called to a position of leadership that he neither sought nor particularly wanted. He was doing what he was comfortable doing. It was safe herding sheep. He had no dreams and no aspirations beyond Midian.

In a wonderful article in *Congregations* magazine from the Alban Institute, Lawrence Peers asks three poignant questions:

1. How often do we prefer the familiar and the safe?
2. How much do we prefer to remain with what is, with no inclination to move toward what is possible?
3. How often as leaders of faith communities do we stay on the edge of our own Red Sea waiting for some miracle to occur before we even budge?

These are important questions we must ask ourselves if we are going to "move beyond Midian" into the future to which God is calling us.

"We need practical directions as we embark on our own expeditions into what is possible," Peers says, "not just for the congregations we lead but also for ourselves as leaders. In fact, for us to effect deep change—that is, change that is not just episodic and on the surface but change that is generative and transformative—we need to re-author our own leadership. In so doing, we are not merely agents of change but, like Moses, we are changed."[1]

Leading change is not just doing something different. Moses did not only lead his people out of Egypt, but he also led them to a new understanding of who they were and of what was possible.

In the late spring of 1986 I was called as the pastor of First Baptist Church in Wilmington, North Carolina. It was a sizeable congregation that ran about 380 in worship. Both the church and I faced a challenge because I had never before been a pastor. For five wonderful years it had been my privilege to serve as associate pastor at First Baptist Church in Greensboro, North Carolina, but I had preached only thirty-one times in my whole life. While Dr. Alton McEachern, the pastor in Greensboro, taught me well, to say that I was in over my head did not begin to capture just how green I was. But the Wilmington pastor search committee felt led by God's Spirit to take a chance on me, and for that I shall always be grateful—to them and to God.

A lot of wonderful things happened during my twenty-five years at Wilmington. While we were an old downtown church with no parking, we continued to grow and thrive year after year. Eventually, at every turn, someone was asking to come visit our church to observe what was happening at old FBC; to come and spend time with our staff and laity. Sometimes it was just the pastor or a staff person. Sometimes it was the whole church staff. One church brought twenty-four people and spent a weekend with us, for the most part just listening to our story.

A few years ago Jim Everette, Jayne Davis, and I were invited by Ron Crawford, president of Baptist Theological Seminary at Richmond (BTSR), to go to the seminary and tell our story as part of the Hoover Lecture Series. I reminded Ron that we were not academics but rather folks who have spent our lives as practitioners of ministry in the local church. He said, "That is precisely why we want you to come to BTSR." Add to Ron's invitation the fact that several other churches were asking to come spend time at Wilmington, and we wondered aloud if maybe we actually had something to offer to the broader church by way of encouragement.

The next year our staff was in a retreat at the North Carolina Baptist Assembly at Fort Caswell. To say that we were in a bit of a funky mood would not quite capture the feelings we were experiencing. With the economic malaise that had gripped the country and in turn our church since 2008, we were simply flat—and a bit unsure of ourselves and of our future. Giving had flattened out. Attendance had flattened out. All of us were flattened out, too. Still, and because we really do believe "the best is yet to be," we began to try to figure out "what next."

At that retreat we considered the notion of offering a one-time conference that told our story to anyone who wanted to come and hear it. As a staff, we anguished over the idea that it might be perceived as self-serving, but in the end we simply wanted to offer encouragement to other ministers and traditional churches like ours. We believed that God was calling us to this unique ministry.

The following October, in 2010, all of those plans came together. In partnership with the Cooperative Baptist Fellowship (CBF), CBF of North Carolina (CBFNC), and The Columbia Partnership, we offered a two-day conference, "Hopeful Imagination: Traditional Churches Finding God's Direction in a Changing World." We borrowed the title, "Hopeful Imagination," from a book written by Old Testament scholar Walter Brueggemann. Those two words resonated deeply with us, capturing much of what we as a staff and congregation had experienced across the years.

In that book, drawing on the previous work of Gerhard von Rad around the poetry of Jeremiah, Ezekiel, and Second Isaiah, Brueggemann said his purpose was to make a contribution to the discussion about vitality in ministry. Early in the book he commented:

> My sense is that the ministry of the American church is in many ways fatigued and close to despair. That is so because we are double-minded. On the one hand, we have some glimpses of the truth of God's gospel . . . and we see where it may lead us in terms of social reality. On the other hand, the church is so fully enmeshed in the dominant values of our culture that freedom for action is difficult. In any case, it is evident that ministry will be freed of fatigue, despair, and cynicism only as we are able to see clearly what we are up to, and then perhaps able to act intentionally. Such intentionality is dangerous and problematic, but when and where the church acts with such freedom and courage, it finds the gift of new life is surprisingly given.[2]

Again and again we found Brueggemann's words to be true for us. By no means were we always as intentional as we could or should have been. We could have taken more risks. We could have been far bolder. But we were an old downtown church in a southern city that was quite content with things as they were, and yet we were able to experience that gift of new life. It soon became obvious that our story, as limited as it was, held some interest for others. We offered the conference for those who were "fatigued and close to despair."

More than 350 people from eight states and several denominations participated in "Hopeful Imagination." Clearly we had touched on a need.

After the conference, people kept asking for the particulars of the story. "You need to write a book," they said. I always contended that I would never write a book, sensing that I had little of value to say to others that had not already been said. But at the encouragement of my good friends George Bullard, Eddie Hammett, Johnny Pierce, and Walter "Buddy" Shurden, here we are. This is not a "how to" kind of book. You do not need or want to be First Baptist Church Wilmington. Rather it is our witness to what God has done in and through this congregation and staff. Our hope is that you will find yourself in the story and catch a glimmer of both hope and imagination for what God wants to do in you and in your church.

One of my seminary professors, Dr. Bob Dale, spoke words that have influenced me throughout my ministry. "Your best ministry," he said, "will come after you have been in a place for at least seven years. Because few ministers stay in one church that long, most of you will never know what your best really is."

Those words haunted me. I desperately wanted to know what "the best" could be.

That gave rise to the question in me: "How do you go to a church and stay forever?"

Prior to coming to Wilmington, I called two respected long-term North Carolina Baptist pastors, Dewey Hobbs and Jim Cammack, and posed the question to them. Both gave virtually the same answers: "First, you have to go to a good church. And second, you have to work hard." I believe they were spot on with their analysis.

As younger ministers have asked similar questions of me, I have added a third ingredient to the mix: "You have to believe that the best is yet to be."

For me, I had to continually look around the corner for what God was going to do next in our congregation. The idea that "the best was yet to be" propelled us forward through the years, as we eagerly anticipated the next new and challenging opportunity God had planned for us.

If you don't believe in the good that is ahead, if you believe that your best days are behind you, then you may as well close the doors to your church. Our God is a God of new beginnings, and he is continually at work.

In order for a church to believe that, it has to have hope—and lots of it. It has to be able to "imagine" a future better than its current reality. And the leader has to believe that the congregation's best days are yet to be. The stories in this book give testimony to those realized hopes. But none of this happened overnight.

Eugene Peterson has written a fine book with an even better title, *A Long Obedience in the Same Direction.* I think it is helpful to recall that title as you "hear" the story of First Baptist Church Wilmington. Where we are today is not where we used to be. It has truly been a journey—and a long one at that—one that I hope has been "a long obedience in the same direction."

As we share this story, it remains our hope that you will have both a realistic and hopeful view of ministry in the local church as we have experienced it. We do not pretend to have all the answers. Our failures along the way have been far more plentiful and of some magnitude. I can assure you that we have learned much more from our mistakes than from our achievements.

While our staff has been privileged to be a part of that story, we are not the only authors. Those folks in our wonderful congregation, along with the eight generations who went before us in the 200-plus-year history of FBC, have invested their lives and resources in this story as much as, if not more than, we have.

None of these stories would have emerged without four key components in the life of First Baptist Church. Each in its own way was critical to what unfolded over a couple of decades.

Openness to Change

First, FBC Wilmington members were open to change—that is, eventually. In time, they were willing to trust the staff and other church leaders. They were willing to take risks and to go to places they had never before been. They were willing to launch new ministries and interact with people very different from themselves. They were willing to sacrificially fund all of these initiatives. And most importantly, they were willing to give their time and energy to serving in the church and in the world.

If your church is not quite so open to change right now, take heart. In the beginning, FBC was not a church that embraced change gladly.

In my first week as pastor, Jeff Lewis, who had been called as minister of music just three months before me, came to me with a question: "Can we sing 'Amazing Grace' this Sunday?" he asked.

He had included the old hymn in an order of service a month or so earlier, but had been told by a church secretary that "we don't do music like that around here."

"Amazing Grace" did not fit with that week's message, but I told him that, when it did, we would sing it. A few weeks later, the hymn seemed to fit so I told Jeff to include it. In great distress, the dear lady who typed the order of service asked me what to do about it. She said she had warned the minister of music about this before. I told her it was fine and that we would sing the song on Sunday, at which point she suggested that I might want to call the chair of deacons for approval. I told her that if I needed that kind of approval, I was probably in the wrong church.

So, "living on the edge," we sang "Amazing Grace" the next Sunday, and from what I could tell, we sang it well, as though we might have sung it somewhere else before.

Emboldened by such "courageous" leadership on my part, I took my next big stand.

It was my first Christmas at FBC. Traditionally, the church held a candlelight Communion service at 11 p.m. on Christmas Eve. Bemoaning the fact that children could not participate in such a late service, I suggested moving it to 5 o'clock. No one was in favor of that. So, in the spirit of Christian compromise, we settled on 7:30, which proved to be the absolute worst time for such a service. Hardly anyone showed up.

One woman, in particular, took me to task over this seemingly minor decision. She informed me that she would be at St. James Episcopal Church on Christmas Eve at 11 p.m., the appointed time when Christmas Eve actually took place. Apparently, many other members of the church joined her at St. James that year, as the next Sunday several of them told me how wonderful the service was. The next year we conducted two services: one at 5 p.m. and another at 11 p.m. We tried to learn from our mistakes.

The new guy was one for two. Fortunately, over time, my average improved.

Openness to change doesn't just happen. It emerges out of trust—trust of God and of one another. You receive a certain amount of trust from the congregation when you walk in the door as the new pastor; the rest of it has to be earned. It is that trust that gives you the right to lead change in a congregation, and earning it simply takes time.

We learned together over the years, the congregation and the staff. We learned to listen to one another, to take chances, to believe that God had something more in store for us, and through us, for the world.

Timing

The second component in our story was timing. What is happening *around* your church is as integral a part of your story as what is happening *in* it.

In the early 1970s, Wilmington experienced the racial strife that infected many southern cities in that era of civil rights struggles: school burnings, curfews, massive arrests. It was not a pretty time in Wilmington's history. Downtown was not always a safe place to be. The church, which had thrived throughout the first twenty years of Randolph Gregory's ministry, began to erode a bit. Evening services on both Sunday and Wednesday were cancelled because of the curfews. A "white flight" to the suburbs was in full motion.

In 1975, led by Reverend Gregory, the church acquired land and built an activities center four and a half miles from the downtown church. It was a controversial move since some members of the congregation wanted to relocate the entire church to the new location, while others feared such a move. That decision to build the activities center and to remain downtown proved pivotal in the emerging future of the church. That same year, with the retirement of Reverend Gregory, the church called Allen Laymon as pastor. With the opening of the new activities center in the late '70s, the church began to stabilize and develop youth and recreation ministries that were unmatched in the area.

My wife Bobbie and I arrived at FBC in 1986, just about the time that the Wilmington Downtown Area Redevelopment Effort (DARE) was beginning to take hold. In the mid-'70s that group began to clean up the urban decay of the historic downtown. By 1986, downtown was finally becoming the place to be—albeit in a way far different from the 1960s. Trendy restaurants began to open, and a vibrant center to our small city began to emerge along the Cape Fear River and throughout the historic district, which included the church property. Then, in 1990, Interstate-40 opened to Wilmington, bringing with it a large number of retirees who came with the incredible ingredients of time, expertise, and resources. That move, along with a host of young people who wanted to live at the beach, transformed the whole community.

FBC was a beneficiary of all of that. We grew as our city grew. Not every church did, though. We worked very hard and with intentionality to reach out and to fold all those new folks into meaningful ministries at FBC.

Staff

The third component of our story is particularly precious to me. All too often I have heard other ministers bemoan the lack of dedication of church members and/or staff colleagues, and that saddens me. The staff at FBC has simply been the best. While we have had a few staff members to come and go, each in their own way made a contribution to our story. But it is the core staff members with long tenures who have helped transform FBC. Part of it has been the result of good chemistry, but, in the end, we were intentional in building trusting relationships.

Sometimes people ask, "Yes, but how did you do that?"

First of all, my office door was always open. The staff knew they had access to me whenever they needed it. And I knew I could walk through their doors at any time, too. We talked a lot with one another and in groups. We were engaged in one another's lives and work.

Second, everyone had an expansive freedom to do their work. Talk to any one of them and they will tell you there were few boundaries when it came to new ideas and/or ministries. They were professionals and were treated as such.

Last, we really did trust one another. That doesn't mean we didn't have differences of opinion, but we were unified in support of one another. More than that, we enjoyed our work, and we enjoyed working with one another. They are my friends with whom I was privileged to minister.

Don Vigus has been a part of the staff for thirty-five years, thirty-two as minister to youth and the last three as minister of recreation and missions. Don possesses the most simple and deep faith of anyone I know. He is incredibly imaginative and fun-loving, generating many a laugh for our staff and endearing himself to two generations of youth and parents.

Jim Everette has served as associate pastor for twenty-one years. He has been my trusted confidant and my loyal friend. He and I shared the bulk of pastoral duties. Beyond that, he led the charge to make us into a missional church—before "missional" was even a word. Jim helped members of our congregation to engage every ministry in Wilmington, which proved to be just as transformational for the church as it was for the community.

Kurt Wachtel has served as minister of music and worship for more than twenty years. Assisted by his talented organist wife, Jean, Kurt planned all of our worship services and led dedicated volunteers in the chancel choir and praise team in such a way that they inspired all of us in worship week after week, year after year. Having a worship leader who is as comfortable directing a thirty-five-piece orchestra and a sixty-voice choir as he is leading a praise band is a blessing to FBC. It was a great time with those three guys.

Jayne Davis joined the staff thirteen years ago as minister of spiritual formation. Her creativity, sensitivity, wisdom, and intellect made us a better staff. She has led members of the church to write all of our Sunday school materials and also a daily devotional. She is also the one member of the staff who had the ability to see the big picture in all we did. She always led us to go deeper in every undertaking. She made us all better than we might have been otherwise.

Jeannie Troutman came on staff at the same time as our minister to children. Her tireless efforts to provide the best learning experience for our children still cause all of us to marvel. She brings people together to craft the most creative ways to share our faith with the newest generations. With the help of many good people, Jeannie completely re-engineered children's ministry at FBC. Our children are being rooted in scripture and the essentials of our faith.

Daryl Trexler, our first-ever minister of administration and senior adults, and Stefanie Riley, our first minister of connections, joined us a few years later. Both of them have proved to be invaluable team members who have brought a new perspective to some of us "older" ministers. These two younger ministers have inspired me to invest a lot of my energies in retirement in the next generation of ministers. They give me great hope for the future of the church.

Frank Hawkins, a retired pastor, has proved to be invaluable as the part-time minister of pastoral care. He has also provided sound counsel to all of us across the years. Amanda Norris capably launched our FBC preschool as its first director. Joe Capell and Vicki Dull have served as excellent executive directors of our Harrelson Center. Our support staff members have supported every effort in the church. They are Tim

Age, Judy Brown, Ashton Gourlay, Michael Gunday, Margaret Johnson, Marie Lane, Paula Philemon, Kelly Reynolds, and Brenda Walden. We could not have accomplished the things we have done apart from their selfless work ethic. No pastor has ever been more blessed by the folks he or she was privileged to work alongside than I was.

The Holy Spirit

Finally, and most importantly, God has blessed this church in ways far beyond our human efforts and abilities. There are parts of this story, as you will see, that cannot be explained apart from the power of the Holy Spirit. It has been incredibly humbling to be a part of this story. To attempt to say anything more about what God has done would be to trivialize it all. It has been a "God thing" for sure—to which the stories in this book will bear strong witness.

Make no mistake, we are all on a journey; we all have our mess, but we also have a word of hope to share. Things will never again be as they once were for most American churches. The world has changed, and the church must change to reach the new world reality. To be missional is to be in the world. This is the calling and the hope of today's churches. Our God is the one who promises to "make all things new"—including the church.

To the best of our ability, Jayne Davis and I have sought to tell the story of Hopeful Imagination at First Baptist in Wilmington. While I have recounted the experiences of our congregation, Jayne has framed each chapter, beginning with a lesson learned from Hopeful Imagination that we believe may have relevance for your church. Then at the conclusion of each chapter she has offered her own reflections on the meaning of the story for FBC along with coaching questions to help you and your church on your own journey of hopeful imagination. As you listen to our story, we hope you will think about your own story. Think about what God wants to do next in your life, your ministry, your church, and your town. We hope this story will encourage others who love their church as much we love ours.

Mike Queen
Pastor Emeritus, First Baptist Church
Wilmington, North Carolina
January 2014

Cultivating Hopeful Imagination

Something has to change for you to go to another place.

This book is about you and your church. Yes, the stories are about First Baptist Church Wilmington, North Carolina, but they are told to encourage you as you look for ways God is at work in your own congregation, and to offer hope and to spark your imagination as you think about the future to which God may be calling you. To that end, we offer the following suggestions for how to get the most from this book.

Prime the pump. Pray that God would guide you to see what he is doing and desires to be doing in you and in your church. Think about your own God stories. What are the best things that have happened in the life of your congregation over the last ten to fifteen years?

God doesn't work in a vacuum. The events and circumstances that have brought you to this moment have shaped you along the way—your identity as a church, your sense of mission and self-understanding. They have uniquely prepared you for something yet to be discovered.

Pay attention to the Spirit. As you read the stories in each chapter, pay attention to how the Spirit is nudging you regarding your own ministry context. Listen for . . .

- Whispers. How is God prompting your imagination?
- Groans: What connections do you make to needs in your church or community?
- Praises: What resources or individuals come to mind that could help you move forward?

The stories in this book belong to FBC Wilmington, but the learnings belong to all of us. Each chapter concludes with a few of those learnings and some coaching questions to help you flesh out what they might mean for you and your church. Find the ones that resonate with you and allow them to be a springboard for further discussion.

Connect the dots. When we want to understand what Jesus is talking about in the Gospels, one of the things we listen for is repetition. If something comes up again and again, we need to pay attention. The same is true as we listen for Jesus' voice in our own stories today.

Think about the "whispers," "groans," and "praises" you heard as you read. Consider which learnings and coaching questions resonated with you and your congregation. Think about the God stories that have emerged in your church over the years. When taken all together, ask:

• What do these stories tell you about your church?
• Where do you see repetition of ideas, themes, or issues?
• What is capturing your imagination?
• Where is there energy?

Identify one or two areas or ideas to focus on initially. Gather a group of trusted leaders and share those ideas. Brainstorm possible paths you could follow to pursue them further. Choose one and move forward, with hope and imagination.

For five years, we have been producing our own Sunday school curriculum at FBC Wilmington. In every issue since we began, the same challenge has been printed in the front of each booklet. I offer that challenge to you now as you embark on this journey of hopeful imagination:

This isn't an exercise.
This is your life, your life with God.
Make something of it.
Expect to be changed.
Expect to change the world.

Jayne Davis
Minister of Spiritual Formation
First Baptist Church
Wilmington, North Carolina
January 2014

Notes

1. Lawrence Peers, "Expeditions into What is Possible," *Congregations* 2010-07-01, no. 3 (Summer 2010): 27.

2. Walter Brueggemann, *Hopeful Imagination: Prophetic Voices in Exile* (Philadelphia: Fortress Press, 1986), 7.

The Unseen Hand of God

You don't know when the unseen hand of God is already on a situation.
Believe that it is.

> For all of our preaching and teaching on the power of prayer and the
> movement of God's Spirit, we often go about the work of ministry as
> if it all depends on us. God is at work in our congregations and in our
> communities, often behind the scenes in ways we cannot see. Some-
> times it takes someone on the outside to help us see that more clearly.

When I answered the phone that Wednesday morning, the
voice calling was that of an older black woman. She identified herself as Evelina Williams and said she had heard me at
the "grand opening" of The Rock Church on the previous Sunday. She
just wanted me to know that she and her prayer warriors had been praying for me and for my church. They had read about us in the newspapers
and heard about us on the radio and television.

In point of fact, the whole town had heard about First Baptist
Church and our efforts to purchase the old county jail. On one city block
in the historic district of downtown Wilmington there were two main
structures: our church and the New Hanover County Law Enforcement
Center. The county had recently built a new jail eleven miles away, so
we inquired about the possibility of purchasing the old jail. After several
conversations with county officials, they invited the church to make an
offer on the building.

It's not that the church needed a jail, but a mentor of mine, Dr.
Alton McEachern, had taught me that a growing church ought to be
like the old farmer—the one who said that he did not want all the land,
just the land that was next to his. We had adopted a church policy that
our trustees would always consider any available property adjacent to the
church. We knew that the jail offered a unique opportunity, though we
were not altogether certain what that opportunity was.

Our initial interest in the jail was the fact that it had eighty parking spaces in an underground garage. The church was desperate for parking. For the 800 folks coming to worship each Sunday morning, we had only twenty-seven spaces in our small parking lot, and twenty-two of those were reserved as handicapped parking. The building itself did not appear to offer much promise. When one walked its halls, you couldn't help but notice the many leaks in the ceiling throughout the administrative space. And it was, after all, a jail.

We assumed that we might have to demolish a part of the building or perhaps the whole structure, believing that renovating it would be too expensive an enterprise. To know for certain, we invited a friend and commercial developer, David Swain, to join a group of our church leaders to tour the vacant jail. Standing in the outdoor atrium—the only "nice" section of the building—we asked David about the costs of demolition. He countered with a question of his own: "Why would you want to demolish this building? It's built like a fortress."

We reminded him of the leaks and the poor condition of the jail cells. He convinced our leadership that those things could be repaired at a relatively low cost. And then he asked the singular question that changed everything: "Mike, if you could fix up this building, how could the church make use of it?"

My mind began to swirl. To this point we had been focused solely on the congregation's need for parking. But David's question opened up a much wider lens. I thought of all the non-profit ministries in our city, good people doing great things who struggle to make ends meet. And in that one unexpected moment, the not-so-clearly defined idea of a ministry center was born. Our staff and church leaders began to contemplate what it might mean to turn this place of incarceration into a place of redemption and hope.

A short time later we invited Dr. Doug Bailey to dream with us about the possibilities for an old jail. Doug had been the rector of Calvary Episcopal Church in Memphis, Tennessee, a congregation that birthed more than ten non-profit urban ministries during his time there. He and his wife, Carolyn, founded the Center for Urban Ministry. Doug also taught urban ministry at the Wake Forest University School of Divinity.

Two things were formative about Doug's time with us. First, his boundless enthusiasm for urban ministry sparked a passion and a hope in us that we could actually make a difference in our community through this ragged old building. Doug understood life on the streets and how difficult it could be for some people. He gave us a dozen ministry ideas just off the top of his head.

But it was the second thing we learned from Doug that turned out to be prophetic in so many ways.

"You have no idea how much resistance you are going to incur when you begin to do the work of God in the city," he said. "You will find out more than you want to know about principalities and powers." He cautioned us about public opinion and what the community would think and say. I remember thinking, "Not us . . . not here."

While we don't use the term "spiritual warfare" a lot, it wouldn't be long before we experienced firsthand exactly what Dr. Bailey was talking about.

So, with reasonable hopes that the building could be renovated and some initial ideas and dreams about the kind of ministries it could house, the church trustees and finance team decided to make an offer on the old jail: $1,000,000— money we did not have.

The offer would be contingent on congregational approval. If accepted, the church would have 150 days to conduct its due diligence; time to evaluate the building to see the extent of repairs needed, time to decide how we actually wanted to make use of it, and, of course, time to find the million dollars to pay for it. There was much work to be done.

By a vote of 3 to 2, the county commissioners accepted our bid. In North Carolina the legal statutes require that the sale of any such public building be subject to an "upset bid," which is altogether proper and as it should be. We were fully aware of this statute and were prepared to engage in a bidding process, if need be, while having an upper limit in mind, beyond which we would not bid.

Once our bid became public, news media made it the story of the week. Some people lamented that if the building was sold to the church rather than to a commercial developer, the county would miss an opportunity to add the property to the tax rolls. Other folks just didn't think a church ought to be able to buy property from the county government.

A couple of local radio celebrities announced that they had learned that the church planned to turn the building into a homeless shelter and soup kitchen. That is when the jokes began.

"If you think we have a parking problem in downtown Wilmington now, wait until the First Baptist Church opens its shelter and soup kitchen. With all those homeless folks lining up their shopping carts side by side, there will be no room for cars."

Every day there were letters to the editor in the local newspaper. It was often the "lead story" on the evening news. To say that it was a brutal process misses the full impact of the attacks on the church.

Finally, on the last day for an upset bid, a local developer made his move and upped the ante. Our member, Claude Arnold, who was handling the dealings with the county for the church, began to make preparation for our next bid. In doing so, he read the North Carolina statutes governing the bid process and realized that the developer had made a slight mistake. The statute requires an upset bid to exceed the original bid by at least 10 percent of the first $1,000 and 5 percent of the remaining amount. Therefore, a valid upset bid needed to be $1,050,050 or more. The developer had bid only $1,050,000—which left his bid $50 short, and therefore, invalid.

The time had run out for any other upset bids, so, "by law," the process was over. The county attorney informed us that the church had just bought ourselves a jail for $1,000,000.

Of course, it was not to be that easy. The local newspaper ran a scathing editorial critical of the county commissioners and county staff. They suggested that if anyone had business with the county, they might want to engage the deacons of First Baptist to do the negotiating for them. In short, the whole thing became even more of a very public and political hot potato.

Though the vote of the county commissioners was legally binding, they refused to sign the documents. In response to political pressure, one of the commissioners called for a re-vote on the matter, resulting in a 3 to 2 decision not to honor the contract with the church. That commissioner was quoted the next day in the headlines of the local paper asking of the church, "What Would Jesus Do?" The situation was more than a mess.

The church staff and leaders did our best to communicate with the members of the congregation what was really happening, what our intentions truly were, and to reassure them that nothing would move forward without congregational approval. Still, reading and hearing stuff like this about our church created a measure of concern for all of us. Had we not had the trust of the congregation, I am not at all certain we could have continued the process. But continue we did.

The county leaders knew that they had a binding legal contract with the church by their original vote, but they chose to ignore it. They could not sell the jail to anyone else while at the same time avoiding the threat of litigation. It began to feel a bit like a stand-off. Word was sent that if the church would simply file a lawsuit against the county, the commissioners would reverse their vote yet again and would sign the contract. Of course, it seemed like that was a tactic to create political cover so they could tell the citizens they were trying to save tax dollars by not going to court in a lengthy trial. We had absolutely no intentions of suing the county. But we did continue to remind the commissioners that they did, in fact, have a legal obligation with the church regarding the sale of the jail.

Time passed and activity and conversation around the sale of the jail simply ground to a halt. The jail sat empty, and it seemed as though nothing at all was happening.

But God was at work in the background, as God often is, and some amazing things began to happen in the life of our congregation and in my life, too—a holy convergence, of sorts. This is, as they say, the "back story."

The Back Story

A few years prior to our efforts to purchase the jail, I had received a call from my friend, Ron McGee. Ron was the pastor of The Rock Church, a Pentecostal congregation in Wilmington. His church had burned to the ground in a tragic fire, and Ron called to ask if his congregation could rent the First Baptist activities center, our second campus that includes a large gym and meeting room facilities, located next to the mall and about four miles from our downtown sanctuary. They were desperate for a place to worship. While I felt for him and his predicament, I told him that church policy did not allow us to rent on an "ongoing basis" to any other organization. Ron understood. I later learned that The Rock had found space at the local community college for worship.

A few weeks passed when Ron called again. This time he asked for a face-to-face meeting. He was really desperate. The community college had so many other events scheduled for its facility that the church was constantly trying to find alternative places for worship. Communicating those frequent changes in location to his congregation that averaged 400 in worship became an impossible task. With emotion etched on his face and trembling in his voice, Ron said, "Mike, as a brother in Christ, I beg of you to go back to your deacons, tell them of our dilemma and make an appeal to them on our behalf." I agreed to do as he requested.

At the next deacons meeting I shared the details of Ron's story, which many of them had already read about in the newspaper, along with his request. One of our deacons reminded the group that, in our last strategic planning process, we had voted to make our facilities more open to the community and to those in need. Another deacon noted that, if we had a fire, we would have our activities center to fall back on—a luxury The Rock did not have. Being the cautious soul that I am, I reminded the deacons that The Rock really did have a very different worship style than First Baptist and that people who saw cars in the parking lot might stop for worship thinking they were coming to First Baptist. Apparently, I was the only one worried about that possibility. After just a few minutes discussion, the deacons voted unanimously to set aside our established policy and to allow The Rock Church to use our activities center on Sundays.

When I called Ron with the news, he shouted, "Hallelujah!" He was one happy pastor.

Ron told me that he thought they would need the facility for only eighteen to twenty months. Some thirty-three months later, The Rock congregation was finally ready to move into their new house of worship. Ron called and invited me to come to the inaugural service to bring greetings and to let the congregation express thanks to First Baptist for making a change in policy for them. I tried to beg off since we had services at nine and eleven with Sunday school in between and it would be challenging trying to get to his church and back before the second service started. But Ron would not take no for an answer. His persistence ultimately changed my life and the trajectory of our church.

Just as Ron had promised, when I pulled up to the front door of The Rock at 10:15 that Sunday morning, an usher was waiting, ready to keep an eye on my car as I hurried inside. Another usher took me down to the front row and, as a soloist finished her song, Ron took the microphone and immediately called me up to the platform. He began to retell the story of the fire and the resulting displacement the congregation had endured. He told of his conversations with me and of the ultimate vote of our deacons. He told of how God had blessed The Rock since that day. Average Sunday attendance had grown from 400 before the fire to more than 650 in those thirty-three months at our place. And on that Sunday morning, there were more than 1,200 worshippers packed into their new sanctuary.

Ron handed me the microphone. I told the congregation how pleased our church was that things had gone so well for them and told them what an encouragement they had been to our congregation over the previous three years. Every Sunday morning we saw their members arrive very early to set up for worship and, when they had finished, they cleaned the building and set it up for whatever we needed for our next event. They had been simply wonderful to work with over those three years, and they made us appreciate our facilities—much of which we had come to take for granted.

As I spoke some final words of blessing and prepared to leave, Ron stopped me and said: "Now before Mike goes, you folks need to remember that this is the man who is the pastor of the church trying to buy the old jail downtown to create a ministry center. You all know we have been praying for him and his church every week because God has given them a vision and they are being obedient to that vision." He then led his congregation in a prayer for our congregation.

When he finished, we hugged one another and he called on those in the congregation to show their appreciation. What happened next was beyond words.

The whole place stood and applauded and cheered loudly and with great energy, except for most of the people seated on the front row—an array of local politicians, including some of the county commissioners. They did not seem to know what to do or how to respond. It was priceless. As I made my way back up the aisle and out to my still-running car, I had my Bible tucked up under my arm. People were shaking my hand, patting me on the back, and giving me high fives. I felt a bit like a rock star, but it was a God thing to be sure.

Ms. Evelina

It was three days later when I got the call from Ms. Evelina. She had been at The Rock that Sunday. She said she just felt the Lord wanted her to call me to let me know that she and her prayer warriors were praying for me and for our church. Having never met the lady, I asked her about her prayer warriors. Who are they? When do they meet? Where do they meet? I learned that she and a group of friends had been meeting at her house at 10:30 every Thursday morning for twenty-two years, ever since she had retired.

Ms. Evelina said she would love for me to come one Thursday and join them, but she knew I was a busy pastor and probably couldn't do that. I told her if I was too busy to meet with people who were praying for me, I was probably just too busy. If it was okay with her, I would be there the next day at 10:30. She cried out with a "Hallelujah!" herself, then told me not to come until 11 o'clock since it took a while to "get started."

No sooner had I hung up the phone than I began to reconsider the wisdom of accepting her invitation. My father used to ask, "Son, do you know what you are getting into?" The answer to that question in this case was clearly "No."

My anxiety level was ratcheted up pretty high the next morning and it crossed my mind to call and cancel, but I sensed that Ms. Evelina was the kind of woman who would not be discouraged and would keep inviting me. To postpone my visit would only delay the inevitable. I had said yes to her invitation, and I would go.

The little white frame house on South 10th Street was just across from a public housing project. There were several cars parked on the street, so I had to park around the corner. As I made my uncertain way to her front door, I asked God to be with me. Apparently, God had arrived before I did. There were some sounds emanating from the house, most of which I was not accustomed to hearing. There's a line in an old Delbert McClinton song that says, "If the house is a rockin', don't bother knockin.' Just come on in." They had obviously "gotten started."

I opened the door and stepped inside. Every square inch of the tiny living room was occupied. A slender, elderly black woman was sitting on a piano bench by the front door. She slid over and patted the other half of the bench as an invitation for me to take a seat, which I did. I'll never forget what I witnessed that day.

Eighteen women (twelve black and six white) filled that little room. Some were praying aloud. Some spoke in tongues. Eleanor, a tall young black woman in a bold yellow dress, stood in a corner and sang with a soulful voice that filled the room and beyond. In another corner was a woman who, from time to time, pulled out a ram's horn, a shofar, and blew on it—loudly.

I was clearly in over my head, with no idea as to what might happen next.

In just a few minutes the room began to quiet down. An older woman sitting in a chair to my left began to speak: "Thank you, Jesus. Thank you, Jesus. He's here. He's here . . ." It was Ms. Evelina Williams.

She thanked me for coming to the prayer gathering and asked me to tell the ladies about our plans for the old jail. I gave them the standard stump speech I had been using with our own membership as well as the dozens of community groups with which we had met in an effort to tell our side of the story and to share our vision.

She then invited me to come and kneel before her so that she could pray for me, and then she wanted me to pray for all of them. I agreed, but asked if we could reverse the order. I was pretty sure that I did not want to "follow" Ms. Evelina when it came to praying. So it was that I took her 84-year-old hands in mine and prayed for all of those ladies; for their faithfulness to that group and for their awesome belief in the power of prayer. Several in the room joined me in praying, too.

Then Ms. Evelina began to pray for me.

"Lord, help this boy." (I was by then well into my fifties.) "He's trying to do your will, Lord, but the devil is working against him. So, Lord, you keep him strong. Don't let him give up. Don't let him get discouraged."

On and on she went. Then all of a sudden she whipped out a little bottle of oil, opened it and anointed me as I knelt before her. When she had finally finished praying, I was no longer kneeling. I had simply fallen into her arms, my face buried in her lap, weeping.

To be prayed for by another is always a humbling experience. It surely was on that day. As is often the case when something wonderful happens in your life, you can hardly wait to share it with someone else. As I made my way back to the church, I called Claude Arnold (the man who had handled the negotiations with the county) to tell him about my encounter. Claude, whose late father had been a Baptist minister, could tell what a moving spiritual experience it had been.

"If my daddy was still here," Claude said, "he would say that you have been *touched*."

Indeed, it felt like I had. But that was only the beginning.

"Lord, Help the Boy"

The team working on the purchase of the deal with the county included Claude, myself, and two other men in our church, Carlton Fisher and Berry Trice. Each of them had a particular expertise for the process. We continued to meet in anticipation that at some point the sale of the jail would proceed, but nothing was really happening. We continued to pray, but with little to show for it. Discouragement had taken hold of all of us, and we began to wonder if all our efforts had been for naught.

From time to time I would receive a call of encouragement from Ms. Evelina to remind me of her continuing prayers. I even stopped by to visit her one day as I was passing near her house and shared with her our discouragement. But this gentle saint simply does not know the meaning of the word "despair." She just smiled and told me to trust God.

"If the Lord wants you to have that building for his work," she said, "you will have it!"

A couple of months passed, and I received another call, this time from an excited Ms. Williams. She told me she had some very good news for me. The Lord had come to her the night before and told her that the church was going to get the old jail! I assured her that we were working diligently on the purchase.

She stopped me mid-sentence, saying, "No Mike. You don't understand. The Lord told me you are going to get it. It will happen, but I have no idea where you are getting the million dollars to pay for it. So that's what we will pray for now!"

While I am a praying person and one who believes deeply in the power of prayer, I have to confess that I was skeptical of Ms. Evelina's claim. It seemed like wishful thinking to me. But, sure enough, the next time I went to visit Ms. Evelina's prayer group, there was no "wishful" about it. They had clearly moved on in their prayers for our church, praying fervently now for the money to close the deal "when" we got the building.

That fall, one of the commissioners who had reversed her vote on our original deal with the county decided to run for a state Senate seat. A new county commissioner was elected to fill the vacancy, and he took office in January. At his first meeting, the new commissioner raised a question as to what was being done with the old jail. The county attorney noted that the county had an obligation to the church, but that they had previously voted not to honor it. The new commissioner made a motion to honor the original deal, and the vote passed 3 to 2. The chair signed the contract on the spot.

After months without movement, our circumstances changed in a single morning. The clock on our 150 days of due diligence had officially begun.

Unable to contain my excitement, I called Ms. Evelina with the good news—only to be greeted with silence on the other end of the phone. I asked her if she had heard what I had said.

"Did I not already tell you this?" she replied calmly.

"Lord, help the boy. Help him learn to trust you, Lord, and only you."

A bit chastened by her words, but most grateful for her prophecy fulfilled, I humbly thanked her for her faith and her prayers. She thanked me for calling and added, "We're still praying about the money." So were we.

A million dollars was a lot of money, especially since our congregation was already in the middle of a $3,000,000 capital campaign to double the size of our activities center. And now the clock was ticking as we worked to pull the funds together.

About two months later Ms. Evelina called and asked if I could stop by her house, which I did later that day. She was incredibly excited as she told me that the Lord had visited her again and had told her that we were going to get the million dollars we needed for the jail.

I reassured her that we were doing all we could to that end by pursuing grants and foundations, talking with banks, and so on. She held up her hand in gentle frustration.

"No, Mike. You don't understand. The Lord told me that someone in your church is going to give you the million dollars. One person will give it all!"

Knowing our congregation as I did, I was fairly certain that was not going to happen. We have some well-to-do members, but a million dollars is a million dollars. Skepticism must have been written across my face. Ms. Evelina charged me not to worry one more minute about the money we did not have.

"God has already taken care of it," she said.

I left Ms. Evelina's home that day convinced that she was an earnest Christian woman, but that she often gave in to outrageous hopes. In my mind she had finally crossed the line of credibility.

A few weeks later, Jim Everette, our associate pastor, came to my office to tell me that a member of the church had asked us to lunch the next day.

"What does he want?" I asked. Jim didn't know, but we agreed to meet Bobby Harrelson the next day.

Over a delightful lunch at an outdoor restaurant on the river, we spoke about all manner of things—sports, business, politics. After the waiter cleared the table, Bobby asked us what we planned to do with the old jail "if" we got it. Jim and I launched into our spiel about the dream of a ministry center.

"I'd like to help you boys get it," Bobby said.

We thanked him and told him that we needed all the help we could get. We went on to tell him about all of our efforts to secure adequate funding.

"No," he said. "I want to help you boys get it. I want to give you the money to buy the building."

Jim looked at him from across the table. "Bobby, the building costs a million dollars."

"Don't you think I knew that before I asked you boys to lunch?" Bobby replied without missing a beat.

People have always wondered what it would take to get two preachers to be quiet. We now know that a million dollars will do the trick. Jim and I were dumbfounded and speechless. We could never have imagined such a gracious offer.

As we tried to get our minds around what had just happened, Bobby reminded us that he was well aware that a million dollars was a lot of money. These words came from a man who was orphaned at a young age and raised by a couple of school teachers in a small rural community in South Carolina. He had come to Wilmington as a house framer and eventually became a successful residential developer.

When I asked Bobby if there were any strings attached, he said, "Oh yes." And then he offered only two.

First, he wanted the building used for "Christian humanitarian purposes." He allowed how that caveat ought to be broad enough so as to not hamstring the work of the center. We certainly agreed.

His second request was more personal. He recalled a church newsletter article I had written in which I said we did not plan to identify the ministry center as just a part of First Baptist. We wanted it to be seen as a facility for the whole community. He then asked if it could be named in memory of his late wife, Jo Ann. She had died of cancer a year earlier. Just before her death, Jo Ann had asked Bobby if they would be able to help the church live out our dream with the purchase of the old jail. He promised her they would.

On my way back to the church, I called Ms. Evelina, who was by now on my speed dial. With great excitement I shared the good news with her. Though I obviously could not see her, I felt her shaking her head through the phone.

"Have I not already told you this? O Lord, when will he ever learn? When is he going to learn to trust you and your promises?"

Humbled beyond belief, I drove to her house. We talked. We prayed. I told her I was sorry that I had not heard her words with the same conviction and assurance she felt. Truth be told, I was not accustomed to having my prayers answered so completely, so directly. My heart felt like it would explode.

Back at the office, I called the three men on the team and told them about Bobby Harrelson's gracious gift. We made plans to convene the next day to begin to work out the details of the process.

Bobby had asked that we not announce "who" was making the gift until the church voted to receive the gift and assume the responsibility of operating and managing the 60,000-square-foot monster that is the jail. At a special Sunday evening called business meeting, the church made that unanimous decision. When Bobby Harrelson was announced as our benefactor and that the building was to honor Jo Ann, those in the congregation rose to their feet in applause, with gratitude and loving admiration. Bobby was emotional and humbled himself. It was a grand moment.

Once all the legal and financial matters were wrapped up and we had actually closed on the purchase of the jail, I invited Ms. Evelina to come and join us in worship one Sunday. The congregation had heard about Ms. Evelina and scattered pieces of the story over the months, but I sensed it would be good for our people to meet her. She and I decided that we would "preach together" on that Sunday. Two of the men had to help her up the steps to the pulpit, and when she got there, she leaned heavily upon it—and on me.

We recounted every detail of our journey together. We spoke a good bit about prayer and about the promises of God. It soon became obvious the love and affection we held for each another. At the end of the first service, I told folks that, if they would like to speak to Ms. Evelina, she would be sitting on the front row as she waited for the second service. As people began to enter the sanctuary for that second service, there were still people from the first service in line to speak with Ms. Evelina. Some came to thank her. Some came to ask for her prayers. One woman brought her three children and asked if she would say a word of blessing over each of them. Many of them knelt before her. She laid hands on all of them.

After the second service, the same thing happened again with the last person rising from in front of Ms. Evelina at 1 p.m. Some left with big smiles. Some wiped away tears. But everyone was touched in some way on that Sunday. For four hours Ms. Evelina had prayed, preached, and blessed the people of First Baptist Church. It was a day no one who was present can ever forget.

Our church was changed, not just by that day, but by all that we had been through. As one woman said to me, "You know, Mike, I really do not believe that there is anything we cannot do with God's help!" That belief is now a part of the DNA of First Baptist Wilmington.

It was a gorgeous fall day when the church and community joined Bobby and his family and friends for the dedication of the Jo Ann Carter Harrelson Center. In his brief remarks, the chair of the county commissioners reflected that it was clearly the hand of God that had brought all of us to this day. He was right. Even then, it truly was just the beginning.

Today the old jail has finally become that place of redemption that was but a dream a few years ago.

The pastor of a congregation is supposed to be a spiritual leader alongside the people. While I had always sought to do that with a measure of integrity and ultimate trust in God, I learned so much more about it from others in this chapter of my life.

From Ms. Evelina I learned the awesome power of prayer and of the need to listen for the voice of God.

From the Harrelson family I learned just how generous people can be when they see a need and feel called to live into a vision.

I learned from members of the congregation that they were more prayerful and patient than I ever knew. They trusted our elected church leaders and staff through a difficult and very public dispute. A lesser church might have crumbled in the crucible.

But in the end, what I learned most clearly was about the power of the Holy Spirit. If any one of the dozens of details in this story had unfolded in a different manner, this story would not have been told.

. . . If Ron McGee had not come back a second time with his request
. . . If the deacons had not said yes to Ron's request
. . . If Ms. Evelina had not gone to The Rock the one Sunday I was there

. . . If Ms. Evelina had not called me to tell about her prayer group

. . . If I had not accepted Ms. Evelina's invitation

. . . If the church had filed a lawsuit

. . . If the church and the leadership team had grown tired and given up

. . . If a new commissioner had not been elected

. . . If Jo Ann Harrelson, on her death bed, had not asked Bobby to help
    make it happen

. . . If our congregation had not trusted us.

The cynics among us might chalk up all of this to chance or happenstance. I cannot. As Jayne Davis is quick to remind us, "What you say 'yes' to matters." Each door you walk through takes you to somewhere new. It was a remarkable privilege to be a part of this chapter in the life of our church. All along the way there were "nudges"—those things that happened that were so far beyond what any of us could control, do, or imagine. Those nudges and these events were surely the work of the Holy Spirit.

In one of our meetings toward the end of the process, Berry Trice, an attorney given to attention to every detail and a constant doubting of pretty much everything and everyone, made a wonderful observation: "All my life I have heard people talk about 'the hand of God' at work in their lives. To be honest, I had never seen it myself. But now I can honestly say that I have been privileged to experience God at work in the most personal and humbling manner."

A lawyer with emotion in his voice and a tear in his eye is a beautiful thing to see. It is a God thing for sure.

Cultivating Hopeful Imagination

Pay attention to the Spirit. As you read this story, what did the Spirit prompt in you regarding your own congregation and context?

• Whispers: How is God stirring up your imagination?
• Groans: What needs in your church or community do you think about?
• Praises: What resources or individuals or opportunities come to mind?

Allow God's dream to unfold. We would love to take credit for the amazing ministry that is the Harrelson Center; to say, "Wasn't that a great idea we had?" But we had no idea what God was up to when we started this journey. Our vision was for parking. God's vision was to turn a place of incarceration into a place of redemption.

How did we get from point A to point B? By not holding too tight to our own vision, by listening to the voices of people whom God put in our path . . . the developer who asked what we could do with the building, the urban ministry planner who dreamed a new future with us, the prayer warrior who received a word from the Lord.

• What vision are you pursuing right now?
• Are you willing to hold it lightly in your hand and allow God to change it into what he wants?
• How might God be trying to make that change already?

Be prepared for the struggle with principalities and powers. We didn't believe Doug Bailey when he said we would struggle with principalities and powers once we were about the work of God in the city. Little did we know.

It would have been easier to play by the world's rules in the acquisition of the law enforcement center—to sue the county, to fight back on talk radio, to ridicule those who mocked God's vision emerging in our midst. There were shortcuts we could have taken had we succumbed to impatience, but they would have left us far short of the end that God had in mind. Had we not trusted God and one another, we may only have had a very fine parking garage to show for our troubles at the end of the day.

The truth is, we settle for fine parking garages all the time. We abandon a fledgling vision at the first sign of struggle when God is calling us to persevere—not just for our own sake, but for the world around us that is often watching. How we conduct ourselves as we go about doing the work of the Kingdom speaks as powerfully to our community as the things we do.

• Where are you struggling right now?
• How are you tempted to give up, to take short cuts, to play by the world's rules?
• What help do you need to persevere?

Trust that God is at work in the background. It would be easy to write off this story as irrelevant to your congregation by making it all about the million dollars. "Sure, we could do XYZ too if we had someone in our congregation with a million dollars."

But the reality is, we bid a million dollars before we knew there was anyone in our midst with the means or the inclination to put such an incredible sum to work for the kingdom. We were more than a year into this process when the tiny seed of a newsletter article and the dying wish of a gentle saint grew to fruition.

Too often we limit what God wants to do in our midst because we can't see how it will happen. Hopeful Imagination is about being obedient to what God is calling us to do that is beyond our ability to accomplish on our own. It's not about the dollar amount or the affluence of the congregation. It is about trusting God to finish the good work he has started, even and especially if we don't know how that will happen.

- What is God nudging you to do that seems impossible?
- What steps can you take in that direction while you wait for God to fill in the blanks?
- What seeds are you planting that may help others to participate in the work?

Look for the hand of God. It is usually in hindsight that we come to see the hand of God at work in our story—if we take the time to look for it. Perhaps the greatest gift that Ms. Evelina Williams gave to First Baptist Church was the ability to see the hand of God in our story in the present—well, mostly in the present. We were always a couple of faith beats behind her.

The Evelina Williamses in our lives are gifts of grace. We don't appoint them; we discover them in our midst. We give them room and allow them in to remind us of God's presence and God's work in us and through us. They give us eyes to see, entertaining angels unaware.

Seeking, discovering, and naming God's action in the stories of our congregation takes intentionality. Seeing the hand of God is like putting the puzzle pieces together, connecting the dots. It is critical theological work that congregations often fail to do. But when we do, when we pay attention and tell the stories, it shapes what our congregations come to believe about the presence and power of God in their midst.

- What are some of the stories of your congregation?
- How was God present in those stories?
- How do you know God was present?
- How do you tell and retell those stories of the unseen hand of God so that they are not only a part of your past, but also inspire your congregation to look for God at work in the present and to empower them for the future?
- Who has the spiritual discernment of a Ms. Evelina in your church?

Realize what you say "yes" to matters. I have come to believe that miracles are less about the big ask and the big answer than about the small decisions and commitments we make each day along the way.

Things that we write off as unimportant often turn out to be very important. Why would a busy senior pastor of a large church take time to go to another part of town to pray with strangers in a ladies prayer group? How could one newsletter article become so transformational? How could a facilities-use decision by the diaconate ultimately change the mission trajectory of a congregation?

We can't say yes to everything, nor can we pretend to know which yes God will use. But we do need to pay attention to the doors that open in front of us and to be wise and humble about which ones we choose to walk through and which ones we say no to. It matters, and rarely in ways that may be obvious to us at the time.

- What invitations are before you?
- What are you too busy for?
- How can you be more prayerful about what you say yes to and what you say no to?

Timing Is Everything

God persists.
Let things simmer.

> We often get ahead of ourselves. We become anxious for plans to unfold on our timetable or feel the pressure to make things happen to satisfy someone else's. We launch ministries before they are ready or put the wrong people in the wrong position, simply because we are desperate to fill the teaching vacancy in the middle school boys Sunday school class.
>
> We all know that God is about more than filling slots or starting programs; we just don't always live and act like we know it. God is birthing his kingdom right there in our midst, right under our noses. May we have the vision to see where it is springing up, the courage to live into it, and the patience to tend it well.

The jail ministry is one of the most significant ministries at First Baptist Wilmington. Looking back, I continue to be amazed at how it all unfolded. With these words, Jayne Davis describes one of the high and holy moments in the life of our congregation:

I honestly didn't know how all of this was going to work: baptizing seven women in a classroom at the county jail with a garbage can and a pitcher of water—not exactly the holy ground you imagine for such an occasion. Three weeks earlier, women from our jail ministry team had led a Bible study on Philip's encounter with the Ethiopian eunuch. Five inmates heard the Ethiopian's question, "What is to prevent me from being baptized?" with a freshness often lost on those of us with the luxury of opportunity, and asked if they, too, could be baptized.

After much prayer and several phone calls, it had been arranged. On Sunday morning, while most of our congregation would be in worship at the corner of Fifth and Market streets, three members of the jail ministry team and I would be at the New Hanover County Law Enforcement Center. Six other inmates had signed up to attend that morning's gathering, along with the five women desiring to be baptized. As we talked about what it meant to surrender our lives to God and the powerful significance of following Jesus in the waters of baptism, two of those six women made commitments to Christ of their own and asked if they, too, could be baptized.

I had very little prepared to say but began by reading Isaiah 43:1-5, inviting the women to hear God speaking, not only to Israel, but also to them:

> The Lord who created you says, "Do not be afraid—I will save you.
> I have called you by name—you are mine.
> When you pass through deep waters, I will be with you;
> your troubles will not overwhelm you. . . .
> For I am the Lord your God . . .
> I will give up whole nations to save your life,
> Because you are precious to me and because I love you and give you honor.
> Do not be afraid—I am with you! . . ."

Troubles these women knew. Deep waters and fear were all too familiar. But that God called them by name, that God would give anything to save them—and already had—this seemed to catch them off guard.

I looked up when I finished reading. It was as if the whole room had melted. In eleven sets of eyes I saw beloved daughters of God, looking back at me, longing to take in every word of affirmation and grace and unconditional love that God through Scripture had to offer. There was a hunger, a softness, tears. I wished every member of our congregation could have been there.

This was their moment: an unexpected surprise borne of years of faithfulness and hope. In truth, they were there. When those in worship that morning were told of the baptisms about to take place at the jail, our downtown sanctuary filled with applause followed by prayers of thanksgiving and protection and strength for these women.

As the seven women to be baptized each came forward, they leaned over the waste basket and felt the cool water of God's grace fall on the back of their head and down their neck. We called them by name and told them they were dearly loved. The words were familiar: "buried with Christ in baptism, raised to walk in newness of life." Perhaps you know the grace of second chances. It was powerful to be with women so ready, so hopeful for a new beginning.

One day in the mid-1990s, Gary Baldwin, a pastor from Burlington, North Carolina, and a friend of mine and Jim Everette's, was visiting FBC. As we were showing him around the church, he noticed the law enforcement center next door. (It's hard to miss. The mammoth brick structure wraps around two sides of the church and is, by far, the ugliest building in all of Wilmington.) When Baldwin found out what was housed in the building, he asked us if we had a ministry in the jail. Of course, we didn't. When Gary asked "Why?" we had no solid answer for him. To be honest, I was a bit embarrassed.

It's not like we had never thought about it before. For years Jim and I had visited the jail when one of our members or their family or friends found themselves in residence there. We parked in the shadow of that building every day when we came to the church office. We had run the idea of a jail ministry up the flag pole a time or two, but the idea garnered little solid interest.

It was the simplicity of Gary's inquiry that caught hold of me. Of course a church that occupies the same city block as the county jail would have a ministry to those housed in it. Why didn't we? A seed had been firmly and deeply planted. It would be hard to look at that building from this point on without wondering how we were going to get that ministry started.

With newfound passion and a sense of urgency, Jim and I brought up the idea of a jail ministry at deacons meetings. We tried to recruit folks to come on board and get the ministry started. Everyone agreed it was important, many were interested, but none stepped up to take the lead. It was even included in one of our strategic plans, but quickly fell to the bottom of the implementation due to lack of leadership.

Clearly, we were not particularly good at casting this vision. We kept running into one brick wall after another. If preaching and prodding could have made it so, the jail ministry would have started a year or two sooner than it did. Thankfully, though, whether consciously or by God's grace, we didn't try to force the ministry's beginnings. We were earnest, to be sure. We could have twisted arms and gotten someone to say yes, but it would have been a mistake.

Too often we get ahead of ourselves and try to launch a ministry on our timetable. We get antsy and "fill slots" instead of waiting for God to raise up the right people for the job—those with passion and experience and a sense of call. We look for leaders who make sense to us, never realizing that God may already be preparing the most unlikely of candidates. We need to be more like Samuel, not settling expediently for one who looks like a king, but patiently and persistently watching and waiting for the one upon whom God has laid his hand.

Then one day it happened. A well-dressed young woman walked into my office. She was a member of the congregation and had something on her mind she wanted to talk about.

"I park on Princess Street every Sunday," she said, "and I walk through the back lot and look up at that building over there," pointing in the direction of the jail. "I just think about the folks who are in there, and here we are right next door. We worship and they can't. We ought to go to them."

As a pastor, you dream about the moment when someone is going to catch the vision you've been nurturing and sharing for so long. High heels and manicured nails amid the orange jumpsuits in the building next door were just not what I envisioned when I pictured that moment.

I affirmed the young woman's compassion and desire to help and told her that we'd been trying for years to get such a ministry started, but to no avail. The look on my face must have given me away. If she was the last reliever left in the bullpen, it was time to call it a game.

Abruptly, she stood up.

"You don't think I can do this, do you?"

"You're not the first person I would have thought of for launching a jail ministry," I replied cautiously.

With that, she leaned over my desk, pointed her finger square in my face and said, "Mike Queen, I am a convicted felon and I know a hell of a lot more about what goes on in that building than you'll ever know. Now do I have your permission to start this ministry or not?"

"Yes, ma'am."

And so it began. One unlikely person became a catalyst for forward motion.

She began to recruit people for the ministry. Several deacons stepped forward, and Jim Everette made the necessary arrangements with the jail. Soon a team of men fanned out across the cell blocks each Sunday morning during our Sunday school hour, sitting in folding chairs, reading the Bible to inmates on the other side of the bars, talking about life and faith and hope, and praying. Within a few weeks, the women had a team of their own to cover the two pods of female inmates.

From inside the jail, the team could see the steeple of our church through the cell block window. The short journey across the parking lot had taken a long time, but we were finally where we were supposed to be.

The jail ministry continued across the parking lot—faithfully, consistently for years. Jim Glass and Bobbie Smith have given primary leadership to this ministry, coordinating dozens of volunteers, encouraging countless inmates as they have transitioned to prison and have, with their teams, been a strong witness for Christ and FBC to the staff and residents at the law enforcement center.

When the county shut down the jail and constructed a new jail eleven miles from the church in the northern part of the county, we had some fear that the ministry might fade as a result of not being located right next door. That location, after all, had made it incredibly easy for folks to participate in worship on Sunday morning and then head to the jail. But exactly the opposite happened. Despite the need to drive to the jail, even more people made a commitment to this ministry.

It was several years after the new jail opened that Jayne and the others baptized those seven women. Two months before that, Jim Everette had baptized two of the male inmates who had been participating in one of our weekly Bible studies. Two of the men on that ministry team, Lee Porter and Carroll Lipscomb, were so inspired by the experience that they asked for guidance on how to counsel any inmates who professed faith in Christ and requested baptism, and for permission to conduct those baptisms themselves. Their request was a beautiful, unexpected moment.

We talk about equipping the saints, but often our imagination is too small. We commissioned teachers to go to the jail, but God had in mind to bring forth several Philips from among us. Two months later, Lee baptized two young inmates in that same classroom over a plain white trash can with a plastic water pitcher filled with mercy and love—holy ground, indeed.

I would have told you that those eleven baptisms over the course of a few months were the most amazing things to come out of our jail ministry since it began fourteen years ago—that is, until one day in court two years ago. Jayne again tells this part of the story.

Elias

The defense attorney used the word "miracle" several times when the decision was rendered. The paralegal cried. The prosecutor talked with some of our church members on the courthouse steps as he left the building, asking if we thought a young man could really change. Perhaps our lack of legal experience made it difficult for us to grasp how unlikely an outcome we had just witnessed. We just knew we had come for Elias, to stand with him and stand for him, for he had become one of our own.

I had never met Elias in person until a few days before his resentencing hearing. Elias had been a part of our Sunday morning Bible study in the county jail four years earlier, before being sentenced to seventeen years in federal prison. One morning in jail, Elias woke up and prayed a simple prayer. "Lord, I want to be saved today. Please send me someone to show me the way." That very morning, Jim Glass came to lead the Bible study. Jim took a special interest in Elias. He was so young, only nineteen at the time. But Jim saw something more in Elias than the counts on his criminal record and took him under his wing. Elias' faith in himself, in his God, and in the future all began to take root and grow.

Elias used the Bible study materials he received on Sundays to teach other inmates in his pod, and he began working on his GED. Soon after he was transferred to federal prison in Kentucky, Elias sent Jim a picture of himself being baptized by the prison chaplain and wrote of the work he was doing, trimming the stray threads off of military uniforms pieced together in the prison factory, carefully preparing them to be sent out.

I sent Elias a note affirming his baptism. He was quick to respond with a note of his own. Mail is an event when you are in prison. His words were grateful and affirming, encouraging and blessing. He spoke of his trust in God in the midst of daily struggles and asked that God would bless me and the church. It was his recurring theme in our limited correspondence: always hopeful, always grateful. I suspect that is what sustains a person facing seventeen years behind bars—what sustains any of us, really.

One afternoon at the church office I reached into my mailbox and pulled out a burnt orange envelope, something from the federal government. The contents looked like a tax refund check, but it was addressed to me personally at the church address. A small amount . . . perhaps it's some kind of sales tax refund from our church bookstore, I thought. I searched the check and summary for clues as I walked to Mike Queen's office. Whatever it was, it was federal and official and I wanted a witness.

As I began to explain the perplexing check in my hand, there I saw it in tiny print. "Tithe," with Elias' name typed next to it. In that split second, the dollar amount on the check didn't change, but it suddenly grew exponentially in value. There is no minimum wage in prison. This was far more than a tithe. In fact, the amount exceeded 50 percent of what Elias could earn in one month of prison work.

When I wrote to Elias affirming his gift and the sacrifice I was sure it required of him to give, he treated it as a matter of course. He wasn't giving back, as if simply trying to repay a kindness shown to him. He was giving forward. First Baptist Church was his church now, and he wanted to be a part of our work.

If Elias was sending his "tithe" to the church each month, I figured the least I could do was to pay him a visit. On a trip back home to West Virginia for the funeral of my uncle, I decided to make the trip down to Inez, Kentucky to the Big Sandy Maximum Security Federal Prison. Working through the prison chaplain there ahead of time, I got all the paper work approved for me to visit. On that Sunday morning I made my winding way down U.S. Highway 23 to Big Sandy, a 1,500-inmate facility built on the site of an old strip mine. Everything about the place was intimidating: from the parking lot to the inner yard to the guards to the watch towers to the razor wire.

In the huge visitation room I was shocked to see only five inmates sitting with family—five out of 1,500! While I had expected dozens of families coming to visit on a Sunday, it became clear that people with long and/or life sentences do not get a lot of visits. Finally, Elias emerged from the doorway, made his way to the control desk and finally over to me. We hugged like long-lost buddies. We took pictures of one another with his "rented" prison camera.

We began the obligatory Q&A about family and home and such. When I asked how he was doing, Elias said that he had not slept the night before. He said he was so nervous about my visit. It was hard to imagine that he was more nervous than I was.

"You are the main man at the church," he said, "so this is a big deal."

As we spoke, I asked Elias if he wanted to be a part of our church. With a puzzled look, he said "I thought I already was. I sent my baptismal certificate, and I send my tithe."

I reminded him that he had never even been to FBC.

"That part is true," he said, "but you all came to me."

For two hours we talked, and then I told him I needed to get on the road for the eight-hour drive back to Wilmington. We joined hands and prayed. As I stood to leave, with widened eyes, he asked, "You're driving back to Wilmington tonight?" When I nodded "yes," his eyes grew even bigger.

"But you will miss the Super Bowl!" he protested.

I told him that I would listen on the radio and hopefully catch the end of the game when I finally got home. He couldn't believe that someone would give up the Super Bowl to come visit him. I couldn't believe that he couldn't believe it. What an incredible day in my life!

The next Sunday I shared the details of my visit to Elias with the congregation. I told about his baptism in prison and his tithe to the church. I told how I had asked him if he wanted to be a member of FBC and of how he told me that he thought he already was.

While certainly unconventional, I suggested that we go ahead and accept him as a baptized believer. Hands raised high in affirmation, brought back down only to enable applause. Few things bring a bigger smile to Elias' face than the fact that his picture appeared with all the rest of the church family in the next church pictorial directory.

It is hard to know who grew more in their faith that day, Elias or our congregation. The jail ministry has been that kind of journey, helping us to discover who we are and finding out that it is more than we thought we could be. Only a few dozen folks have participated in the jail ministry over the last thirteen years, but it is a part of our identity as a congregation. "We" are the church that goes to the jail. And now the inmates at the jail, in a mosaic that forms the face of Elias, are no longer an anonymous "them," but have become part of "us." That seems as it should be.

It's not unusual for one person's story to shape the narrative for the whole. Our hearts don't connect to a big picture; they connect to another's heart, another's story, and therein we find ourselves.

As is God's way, the more we have come to know Elias as an individual, the more he has come to embody a bigger story of redemption and second chances, of struggle and hope; of childlike faith emerging against the odds, like a dandelion coming up through a crack in the sidewalk. And we dare to hope that there is enough space in that crack for us as well.

Elias is just a young man who messed up and is finding his way. He is neither a saint nor a hero. He bears no responsibility for our salvation and yet somehow, by journeying with him, we keep stumbling across Jesus along the way.

Once again Jayne picks up the narrative.

"Walking in Victory"

I'd never been on the second floor of the new law enforcement center. The classrooms used for Bible study are on the main level. After I left my only posses-sions—my keys and my driver's license—in the small metal box on the deputy's desk, he pointed me toward the elevator, gave me some directions, and handed me a single key attached to a long wooden stick—like the restroom hall pass from the second grade. I may as well have been eight years old on my way to the store by myself for the first time walking down that long, stark corridor, seeing no one, but sure someone at a monitor somewhere was seeing me. The theme song from "Get Smart" played insistently in my head as each door I passed through closed behind me, until I finally reached the one marked "H."

Through the wired glass window in the attorney meeting room, I met Elias for the first time. He had been brought back to New Hanover County for a resentencing hearing. A higher court ruled there had been discrimina-tion in the sentencing structure for cases such as that of Elias and therefore they must be resentenced.

We had prayed for Elias to have the strength to persevere through the seventeen years of his sentence, hoping that with good behavior it would be a bit less than that. It never occurred to us to ask for more. Fortunately, God has a bigger imagination than the limits of our prayers. At a minimum, under the new guideline, Elias' sentence would be reduced to ten years—an incredible gift! But, then again, when have you ever known God to settle for anything minimum?

Through the black phone on the wall, Elias and I told our stories of family and life and what had brought us to two different sides of the same glass window. As the conversation moved to the upcoming hearing, he said that his attorney was hopeful that he might get seven years. I could tell Elias wanted less, but the judge had a reputation for being tough—which kept a lid on his attorney's optimism, but not Elias'.

"Who knows?" he said. "This might just be the day God wants to move in Judge Fox's life. God does stuff like that to folks, you know."

From all I had heard about the judge's courtroom, it was a long shot. But Elias told me he was "walking in victory" and he believed he would be out in less than a year. I faithlessly tried to protect him from disappointment by reminding him of the incredible gift of seven years compared to seventeen, a miracle I could actually wrap my head around.

Elias quoted the apostle Paul and made a believer out of me, that he truly was ready to be content in any situation, whether he left the courtroom a free man or whether God wanted to work for another three years to get him ready. To live is Christ; to die is gain.

"Either way it will be good," he said, "because it will be God's doing and God will be in it."

Somewhere in the back corner of that tiny attorney meeting room, I am certain I heard Jesus whisper, "Amen."

Elias' case was third on the docket that Tuesday morning at the courthouse. It had not gone well for the two men before him, each receiving the maximum sentence allowed. Elias' case was introduced with the obligatory legal rambling followed by words of gratitude from Elias to the judge and a request to be shown mercy. Ten of us from First Baptist Church stood on Elias' behalf. His attorney introduced us each by name and told the judge we were Elias' new family and friends, a sign of his new life—though who has actually brought new life to whom is an argument for another courtroom.

With little other fanfare, weeks of anticipation unfolded in ten short minutes with four quick surprises:

1. The attorney successfully argued a point of evidence that brought Elias' case down to an even lower tier in the sentencing structure: 61-90 months.
2. At a bench conference the prosecutor unexpectedly agreed to the middle of the sentencing range: 75 months.
3. The judge then pronounced sentence at 61 months, the absolute minimum.
4. The judge waived Elias' fine: $0.

I was running the numbers in my head. Elias had already served forty-four months. In less than a year and a half, I thought, he will be free! We moved quickly to the side of the courtroom where they were taking Elias back into custody so we could wish him well before he left. He smiled with both thumbs up and told me, "I'll be out this year!" as he walked out the door. His math was a little hopeful, I thought—the kind of calculating I use in my head when I want to buy something I can't afford.

As the ten of us gathered with the stunned attorney and tearful paralegal outside the courtroom, I got a lesson in prison sentence math, and learned that Elias' calculations were exactly right. He would be out within the year, just as he had told me the day before—walking in victory.

As we walked down the hallway on our way out of the courthouse, I turned to Wanda Porter, one of our deacons and an original member of the jail ministry team, and asked, "Wanda, could you ever have imagined something like this when the jail ministry first got started?" "Never," she said.

Elias was sent back to Wilmington upon his release. For several weeks he lived at a halfway house. Jayne had reminded us all along the way that the true test for the church would come when Elias was free. Where would he live? How would he make his way in the world? Indeed, the lingering question in the back of everyone's mind was "how will he avoid ending up back in prison?"

It was here that Jim Everette stepped up, along with a bunch of folks in the church. Jim Glass, who had been walking this journey with Elias for years, and his wife Peggy opened up their home to Elias. Doug gave Elias a job at his car dealership. Rob eventually rented Elias a house near his work. People helped with furniture. Greg, a dentist, gave him a new tooth in the place where one was missing. A young adult Sunday school class welcomed Elias. He has read scripture in worship.

While having lunch with Elias one day, he told me the story of his first Sunday school class Christmas party. He went into elaborate detail about the gift exchange and how people could steal another person's gift. He thought it was hilarious. He had never experienced a party like that, something most of the rest of us take for granted. He looked across the table and said, in his sometimes difficult-to-understand tempo, "Man, when I was at the party, I thought for the first time, I am really free." Who knew that was what it took to feel free?

Who Could Have Imagined?

"No eye has seen, no ear has heard, no mind has conceived what God has prepared for those who love him" (1 Cor. 2:9).

To be honest, I could never have dreamed that the jail ministry would have lasted as long as it has, and that so many people would be involved. Sustaining ministry—difficult ministry—can be a real challenge. There was no master plan when we began, but clearly the Master has been at work. But the first step across the parking lot was on us to take.

Sometimes the first step is harder than it looks, but nothing happens until you take the first step.

Our dreams are rarely big enough to contain the things God wants to do. We think too small. We think about what is possible, what we can do. God is far more creative. We just wanted to send folks to the jail, to visit those in prison right next door; to offer encouragement, heal some of the hurt, share a word of hope. God wanted to set the captives free—and us, too.

Who could have imagined . . . that Cory, one of the young inmates, who moved on to a federal prison in Pennsylvania, would mentor a gang member who wanted to change, watch someone he led to Christ be baptized, write a devotion for our church on forgiveness, and write a letter to our congregation exhorting us to fully staff the Saturday jail ministry team because of the difference one man coming to the jail made in his life?

Who could have imagined . . . that a simple email prayer list would become a conduit for outreach and hope? After each visit to the jail, the prayer requests of the inmates are shared by email with folks in the congregation who have a passion for the jail ministry and have committed to pray. One day Les shared a prayer request from one of the men who was concerned about his girlfriend and was hoping someone could make contact with her. Ann saw the email and found a way to contact Shaketta, someone she had never met or spoken to, and offered her a word of encouragement and an invitation to join her for worship. Shaketta rode a bus halfway across town to be with us in worship that Sunday.

Who could have imagined . . . that Stephanie would be released from prison and launch a ministry for women looking to start a new life after being incarcerated . . . that David would get to lead a dying inmate to Christ as they walked together on the roof of the jail . . . that Wanda would get so much mail from prison that the mailman thought her children were incarcerated . . . that the inmates would be Jim's strength and support and encouragement during his son's illness . . . that the coordinator at the jail would light our Advent wreath candle of hope during worship . . . that eleven inmates would be baptized in a classroom over a garbage can or that we would witness a miracle in federal court?

Who could have imagined . . . that Bobbie, Terri, Frances, Wanda, Connie, Ann, Clara, Hazel, Robin, Phyllis, Rebecca, Jim, Lee, Jack, Thomas, Lyn, Les, Carroll, Sean, Rob, David, John, Jay, Austin, and many more good folks would give of themselves so fully, keep in contact with inmates as they move on to prison, give tough love in hard times and gentle grace all the time, and help them to get settled when they are released . . . or that Elias, himself, would return to the jail to lead a Bible study every Thursday night? They actually turned Elias away the first night he went to the jail to teach because his paperwork hadn't been fully processed.

"How ironic is that," he said afterwards. "I went down to the jail, and they wouldn't let me in!"

We could never have imagined it, any of it, but God could—and does—every day. If we had had a master plan for the jail ministry at its beginning, it would have been all about transforming the inmates. But the reality is that God is transforming First Baptist Church through this ministry because we keep meeting him there.

"I was in prison, and you visited me."

The blessing was right next door all along.

Cultivating Hopeful Imagination

Pay attention to the Spirit. As you read this story, what did the Spirit prompt in you regarding your own congregation and context?

• Whispers: How is God stirring up your imagination?
• Groans: What needs in your church or community do you think about?
• Praises: What resources or individuals or opportunities come to mind?

Wait for the right people and the right time. The easiest way to kill a ministry vision is to give it to the wrong person at the wrong time just because you are desperate to get it off the ground. We get caught in the trap of trying to "fill slots" to staff a ministry instead of seeking and waiting for those with the passion, experience, and sense of call that are truly needed.

God's timing and the leaders God raises up don't always make sense to us or fit with our imperfect understanding of what needs to happen. The woman who came to Mike's office was an unlikely candidate in our minds to lead the jail ministry, but it turned out she was the perfect catalyst to get it started.

It was very tempting to try to "make" the jail ministry happen as days and months of wanting it to be gave way to years. But if we had forced it into existence, it probably would not have become such an important part of the DNA at FBC.

• What ministry are you anxious to launch?
• Are you trying to force something that is not ready?
• What positions do you feel desperate to fill?
• How can you be more like Samuel in your search for the right person?

Be aware of opportunities right where you are. Your church probably doesn't need to start a jail ministry. We did, because that was the need right there under our nose.

God has a purpose for our congregations in the places where we are located. Too many times we try to replicate the good things that are happening in other congregations, thinking they will have a good outcome for us. Sometimes that can work. But all too often when we are looking at what everyone else is doing, we miss the opportunities God has uniquely positioned for our own church—the ones right next door.

Whether your congregation is big or small, urban or rural, rich or poor—God has a purpose for your church that no one else can live into like you can.

- What is in the shadow of your steeple?
- What is "right next door" to your church, so close that you can't even see it—the faces, the needs?
- What first step would help you to begin to make your way "across the parking lot"?

Whatever It Takes

Learn from those who free you up to think differently.

There are people we encounter in life who make us want to be better, who dare us to long for something more. It may be their stories or their enthusiasm that capture us. Maybe their resilience or their imagination inspires us. But somehow, through them, God takes hold of us and turns our face to catch a glimpse of something more that he is calling us to do or to be.

It is the same for churches—or it should be. Other congregations can be a catalyst for our own reimagining of what kind of church we are to be.

Who are your conversation partners in ministry? Too often we only listen to folks just like us, in churches just like ours. If we are going to be the church God is calling us to be, we may have to stretch out of our comfort zone and pay attention to some unlikely ministry guides along the way.

Given the choice, I never would have looked to Flamingo Road Church (FRC) for help or guidance. It is nothing like First Baptist Wilmington—nothing. But George Bullard, a consultant with The Columbia Partnership, said he thought it would be good for me to hear a different voice. I had no idea just how different he meant.

If the non-descript building and the rock band leading worship weren't far enough removed from our Gothic sanctuary and chancel choir, the bumper stickers on cars in the parking lot as I pulled in for a week-long conference convinced me that clearly Match.com had gotten this pairing terribly wrong.

"Flamingo Road Church," the colorful stickers read, "Making It Hard to Get to Hell from Ft. Lauderdale, Florida."

"Oh, that will go over big at home," I thought.

We were at one of those "what next" moments in the life of our church when George suggested a visit to Flamingo Road and its pastor, Dan Southerland. Twice a year the church offered a conference on "Transitioning," or leading change in a congregation. I signed up and made the trip to Florida at George's behest. Most all ministers who go to a continuing education seminar or conference hope to bring home at least one idea they can use in their setting. But few among us can say our lives were changed at such a gathering. Mine was.

Along the highways of South Florida there are lots of big churches with imposing structures. Flamingo Road was not one of them. Though housed in what was nothing more than a gym with a stage, a few offices, and a children's preschool area, I knew this congregation was special the minute I pulled into the rather modest parking lot. Not a very "churchy-looking" place . . . and yet it hinted of holy ground. I felt cared for and prepared for.

Members of the congregation warmly greeted each of the 200 or so participants and patiently guided us from the parking lot to the registration area and then to the gym. A very lively praise band was warming up, so I found a seat on the back row, left corner, close to the door. The place was welcoming, to be sure, but I was still uncertain as to whether this would be worth my investment of time and money, so close to the door seemed a prudent location.

After a couple of rousing praise songs, done very well, Pastor Southerland welcomed all of us. Then he did the most amazing thing I have ever seen or heard at such a conference. He told the story of coming to be the pastor at FRC and of how he almost killed the church. What followed was a litany of all the mistakes he made in trying to lead change. With tears in his eyes he told about his best friend leaving the church, along with many others including the chair of the committee that had called him. It was a sad and brutal story.

Dan was young when he came to FRC after having served another congregation as a youth minister. He thought he knew what was best for the church. He had a vision, and a fine vision it was. But, by his own account, he went about implementing it very poorly. He and the church paid a high price in lost members, broken hearts, and hurt feelings. There was "blood running in the aisles," he said.

Dan's transparency in describing his failure was disarming, and it provided the first of many indications that transparency was a key part of the DNA of Flamingo Road Church.

As my late father used to say, "There is nothing all that bad about making a mistake—as long as you learn something from it." Clearly these folks had.

At a staff retreat, lamenting the reduced state in which they found themselves, Dan and his colleagues experienced what can only be described as brokenness. Realizing that they had put their agendas and desires ahead of all else, they humbled themselves and sought the face of God. How all of that unfolded is Dan's story to tell. But the result was a church that, by the time I came for the conference, was running five weekend services and changing lives by the hundreds. The organ had been removed, and praise music was the only option for worship. Plaid sport coats and creased slacks had given way to camp shirts and jeans. The "transition" was in full force.

What Dan promised us over the next few days was to share what he had learned in this painful process of transition. He used the stories of Ezra and Nehemiah and the rebuilding of the walls at Jerusalem as the texts for the week. That ancient story generated a pathway for transition that I am convinced works just as well today.

Each session of the conference offered some new insight into the best ways to lead change in a church. I took notes on everything. Dan fleshed out the rest of his story. He really did make a mess of things, but he always reminded us that "God is good." It took a lot of humility and courage to tell the details as he did, but in every instance he also told of how God redeemed it all. It was inspiring. It was also sobering. There is a price involved in leading change.

"You are going to lose some people if you change, but you will lose others if you don't change," Dan said. "You just have to decide which group you are willing to lose."

That was a terribly difficult word to hear as a pastor. You never want to think about losing anyone. We've heard similar advice over the years from Eddie Hammett, a church coach and consultant with CBFNC.

"If God wants to move people out of your church," Eddie says, "let them go." He agrees with Dan Southerland, who reminded those of us at the Transitions conference, "The work of Jesus is just too important to worry about trying to make everybody happy." They are right.

Dan and the staff were wonderful. At the end of each session when most everyone was scrambling for a snack or a rest room break, they would sit on the edge of the stage and make themselves available to anyone with a question. When I finally got my minute with Dan, I told him a little about our congregation. At that time we were a 195-year-old church in a 140-year-old sanctuary. We preached in robes and lit candles at each service. We were running 700 in worship, and we had no parking.

I shared with him a bit about the "what's next?" question that had prompted my attendance at the conference. He called it a "holy discontent with the status quo." It is what fuels vision, he said: that restlessness with business as usual. It rang true. "Holy discontent" captured where we were as a staff—certainly where I was in my own internal wrestling with what I wanted my ministry and our church to look like. I asked Dan if he had any advice for a church like ours. His words continue to guide our thinking, even to this day.

"The older the church, the slower you go."

That's all he said. I think I was hoping for some shortcut on the journey, some instant clarity to where all of this was leading for First Baptist Wilmington. But in the end, those few simple words were exactly what I, and we, needed to hear. We recalled them often over the years that followed. They saved us much heartache, helping us to avoid the bad decisions that come when doubts creep in and anxiety wants to take over, whispering deceitfully that we needed to be moving faster than we were.

"The older the church, the slower you go" became our mantra.

As great as Dan and his staff were, it was the lay people I met at FRC who captured my heart and fueled my imagination. Three of their stories, in particular, made me wonder aloud if church could really be like this. They painted a picture for me of whom and what I was beginning to hope our church could become.

The Cotton Ball Club

The first person was Mary, a woman nearing seventy. She was invited to the platform to give her testimony. Here is the gist of what she said:

> My husband and I have been members at Flamingo Road for fifteen years. We were all excited when Dan came to be our pastor. But then things began to change. The music, the way people dressed, everything changed. Then our friends began to leave the church. We began to consider such a move ourselves. But something kept us around for a while longer.

After a while, we began to see all these younger people coming to church: young families with children, young singles, and a bunch of people who were not Christians but who became Christians. We were baptizing people left and right. The church was growing, but the music was just awful. My husband and I found ourselves in a quandary.

There seemed only one thing for us to do. My husband and I, along with a few of the older members who remained, formed the Cotton Ball Club. We are here every Sunday as ushers and greeters. Some of us work with the crowded nursery. But when the music starts, we all put cotton balls in our ears to drown out the sound. When the sermon starts, we take them out, and when it's over, back in they go.

You see, I hate this music, but I love seeing people come to faith in Jesus Christ more than I hate this music.

Mary was simply the first person I met at FRC who lived into the motto and mantra of the church, which was spelled out on the dark blue t-shirts they all wore as they guided and served us over the four days we spent with them. In big letters splashed across the back of their shirts was the acronym, WIT, with the T being in the form of a cross. I remember thinking that it must be short for "witness." In a way it was: WIT . . . Whatever It Takes . . . to help people come to faith in Jesus Christ. It was not just a motto. I met a whole church full of folks like Mary who would do whatever it takes to meet whatever need they saw.

An Unlikely Children's Minister

"Jenny" came to FRC under the strangest of circumstances. Long addicted to drugs and willing to do all the sordid things one does for a fix, Jenny had stolen some pills from a pharmacy. Disgusted with her life and what it had become, she took all the pills on a rainy Saturday night and crawled into one of the big concrete culverts by the highway . . . a dry place where she could die. Only she didn't.

Waking that Sunday morning, she stumbled from her would-be coffin. Blinded by sunlight, her mind fogged by drugs, Jenny was a mess standing by the road. All of a sudden a car came up beside her, and the door flew open. It was a woman with whom she had worked years earlier.

The woman called Jenny by name and pulled her into the backseat of her car. The woman's husband turned the car back on to the road.

Too weak to physically resist, Jenny simply asked, "Where are we going?"

"To church," came the reply.

Jenny had no intentions of going to church. That was the last judgmental place she wanted to be. She thought her old friend to be crazy. Finding herself too weak to protest, Jenny laid down in the back seat. She was taken to church, given a cup of coffee, and was warmly greeted by a few folks as she sat with her rescuers. She said she recalled very little about that morning, as she told us her story, but after church the woman and her husband took Jenny to their home, fed her, helped her get a shower, and put her to bed.

That might be a fine story if it ended there, but it didn't. The couple got Jenny into a rehab facility. When she completed the program they took her back into their home and back to Flamingo Road Church. Over time, Jenny heard the gospel. More importantly, she saw the gospel lived out in the lives of others at FRC. Finally, Jenny chose to become a Christ-follower herself and was baptized at FRC.

As it is with all the members at Flamingo Road, Jenny was encouraged to pray for God's leadership and guidance to find a ministry for which she was suited and called. She did that and told Pastor Dan that she felt certain God wanted her to work with the children of the church. Can you imagine? Here was a woman with a questionable past and with a possibly lingering drug problem, and she wanted to work with children. Everyone in the church knew her story. How would parents react? What about liability? A decision had to be made.

Dan counseled her. They made arrangements for her to serve, always with someone else present. They paid close attention to Jenny and to how she was conducting her life. They were not reckless, but they were careful. In the end, Jenny became a part of the staff at FRC. Talk about a transformation and transition! But as wonderful as all of that was for Jenny in her own life, the people at FRC began to realize what it meant for them, too—to not only believe in redemption, but also to practice it.

When I told Jenny's story to the folks at FBC Wilmington, I asked this question: "Do you think we could ever call a former addict to be a children's minister?" "No," I said, in answer to my own question, "at least not today."

But I was beginning to get a vision of the redemptive congregation that I hoped we could become someday—radically redemptive, Jesus' kind of redemptive.

Billy

Despite being slowed by a rather severe physical disability, "Billy" was relentless in serving the conference attendees. He embodied the "Whatever It Takes" spirit, working so hard and with such great effort that I thought he was a member of the church staff. I was surprised when he told me he was "just a volunteer," and asked him how he came to be a member at Flamingo Road. Billy had a story to tell.

The third of four children, Billy's parents always referred to him as the "sick one." He was treated differently from his siblings. When it came time for college, his parents wouldn't help him with the costs—something about him never being able to do anything. Billy withdrew into himself. Jobs were hard to come by, but one day he got lucky. A local gym was looking for someone to work the counter. Billy got the minimum wage job.

One of the perks of the job was that Billy could work out anytime he liked. The end result was amazing. Since his legs did not work like most folks' do, Billy focused on his upper body. From the waist up, the man was rock solid. People at the gym marveled at his dedication and work ethic. It wasn't long until he was training others. He had found a place where he was accepted and respected.

One of the members of the gym was a staff minister at FRC. Every day he was at the gym he invited Billy to church. Billy never went. His family members were all Christians, but the rejection he had felt made him wary of anyone claiming to follow Jesus.

But the minister never missed an opportunity to invite Billy, and Billy never gave FRC a second thought.

Then one Saturday night Billy was driving down Flamingo Road. The next thing he knew, he said, he was in the turn lane that led to the church. He had no idea how he got there. As he told me his story, he asked, "Do you think that was God?" I told him I was pretty sure it was. Once in the parking lot, Billy got out and made his way into the crowd gathering for worship. He took a seat on the back row, left side, near the door—a popular seat for skeptics.

Determined to get out as quickly as he could after the service, Billy planned his getaway. But just as he got to the door, the minister from the gym put his hand on his shoulder and told him how good it was to see him. Billy smiled, but quickly refocused on getting out of the building. Before he could get away, the minister invited Billy to go have dinner with him and some of his friends. They would not take "no" for an answer.

It was the first time since becoming an adult that Billy had ever eaten in a restaurant and not been alone.

Billy told of his anguish of being in high school: the whispers behind his back, the pointed fingers, the cruel nicknames thrown his way, the fact that he had never had a date. Little changed when high school ended. Billy's pain was written into every pore of his face, yet he didn't seem sad or down about his situation in life. Flamingo Road Church was the main reason for his hopefulness.

He could not say enough about the other people he had met there. Deep friendships developed over time. Billy was given responsibility in the church. He said he felt so blessed, so much so that he scheduled his only two weeks of vacation each year to coincide with the Transitions conferences so that he could be available to help out.

The self-sacrifice of the Cotton Ball Club, the redemption of a children's minister, the valuing of Billy . . . My heart was full and overflowing. I was excited, but had no idea where all of this was going to take us at First Baptist Wilmington.

Never Be the Same

And then it crystallized one night for me during the conference when the praise team put on a concert that was open to the community.

The music at Flamingo Road was the same music I had heard in other places, but it "felt" different there. Everyone in the band at FRC was a member of the congregation. For the most part they were people who had not played an instrument since high school, but who took it up years later for the glory and worship of God. The music they played and sang stirred something deep within me. Those folks seemed to truly worship God with their music. Perhaps that is why none of the other bands I heard seemed to rise to the level of the praise team at FRC.

The night of the concert, the gym-turned-sanctuary was packed with conference attendees and others from the community. There were no FRC members in the audience; their role was simply to serve as greeters and ushers and such. While I confess that I was caught up in the sheer energy that filled the room, I took time to look around at the people who had come that evening. There was enthusiasm and joy on every face.

The woman sitting next to me had brought her two young children to the concert. At one point she turned to me and said, "My kids just love this place so much." And then she wistfully added, "Our church would never do something like this." In that moment I wondered if ours would.

Later that evening the band played a song by Australian lyricist Geoff Bullock. While the young woman who sang it had a wondrously powerful voice, it was the lyrics that captured me. They described in full exactly what I was feeling both emotionally and spiritually. Here are some of the lyrics:

I will never be the same again,
I can never return, I've closed the door
I will walk the path, I'll run the race
And I will never be the same again.

(Chorus)
Fall like fire, soak like rain,
Flow like mighty waters again and again.
Sweep away the darkness, burn away the chaff,
And let a flame burn to glorify your name.

There are higher heights, there are deeper seas,
Whatever you need to do, Lord, do in me.
The glory of God fills my life,
And I will never be the same again.

As I listened to the song, tears began to fill my eyes. They overflowed and ran down my cheeks, but I didn't care. I knew in that moment that I would never again be the same. It was pure, raw worship, and the flame of my faith reignited. There was more than one way to be and do church.

Again and again, I repeated those words as I fell before God: "Whatever you need to do, Lord, do in me." My life had changed forever. If I am honest, I didn't like how out of "my" control it felt. But I knew the Spirit was somehow carrying me along.

As we prepared to leave the conference, Dan offered us a word of caution: "There is one more thing you need to remember. Satan doesn't like it when you try to be faithful to God's calling. The more faithful you are to that calling, the more resistance you are going to experience." He did not overstate that reality. Spiritual warfare would become an unexpected part of our story.

Even after a dozen years, Flamingo Road still comes up in our conversations with one another. We are still inspired by that church's story. The people weren't perfect, and we didn't come away with a desire to become or to look like their church, but they rekindled the flame of ministry within us. They gave us a vision of what might be different for First Baptist Wilmington in our future. That experience changed us and shaped us, as a staff and as a congregation, and opened our eyes to the possibilities that God was more at work among us than perhaps we had dared to realize. FRC gave us hope and imagination.

Cultivating Hopeful Imagination

Pay attention to the Spirit. As you read this story, what did the Spirit prompt in you regarding your own congregation and context?

• Whispers: How is God stirring up your imagination?
• Groans: What needs in your church or community do you think about?
• Praises: What resources or individuals or opportunities come to mind?

Allow holy discontent with the status quo to fuel vision. Holy discontent . . . it's not simple restlessness, but a nagging sense that there is something more ahead: a calling, a hope, a change somewhere around the corner. It is illusive and unsettling. Whereas before it had been energizing, business as usual now leaves us a bit empty.

Dan Southerland says that a holy discontent with the status quo is what fuels vision. It's the "what's next?" question that we were wrestling with at First Baptist.

If you are in such a moment of holy discontent, embrace all of its awkwardness and discomfort and the chaos it causes within you. Don't dismiss it or try to resolve it too quickly. Look for God, not just answers. God's up to something, and you get to be part of it!

In his book, *Transitioning*, Dan Southerland says, "You don't find vision when you search for vision. You find God's vision when you search for God."[1]

- Where is a holy discontent emerging in you? In your ministry?
- What is it about the status quo that God may want to change?
- What might that look like?
- How can you let your holy discontent deepen your search for God?

Be a learner. Who are your teachers? To whom are you listening? Often our conversation partners are folks just like us in churches just like ours.

Flamingo Road Church had a heart for reaching unchurched people. The entire congregation was willing to do whatever it took so that hurting people could come to know the hope and healing of Jesus Christ. That is what bonded us to them. That is what inspired us. That is why, more than twelve years later, we still consider them an integral part of our faith journey at First Baptist Wilmington.

If we had dismissed the folks at FRC as having nothing to say to us because of their size or worship style or facilities or socioeconomics or theology, we would have missed a defining moment for our pastor and for our church—a God-given moment that remapped our future.

Sometimes it is exactly because a person or a church is so different from us that we are able to hear God in their story. We are not distracted by thoughts of how we can replicate this or copy that. We are simply present and attentive and are able to listen to God's Spirit amid all the words and activities.

We still look nothing like Flamingo Road Church. But because of that congregation, we are more fully and authentically the church God has called First Baptist Wilmington to be.

- From whom would you most like to learn?
- What voices do you resist hearing?
- Who can help you to identify a conversation partner with a much different voice than your own?

Look for God's face in your congregation. Seminars are great. How to's are helpful. But stories are powerful.

Mary and Jenny and Billy gave us glimpses of the face of God in Flamingo Road Church. Not because they were perfect, but because, in them, we saw self-sacrifice and redemption and belonging. In them we saw Jesus.

But their stories did something else to us. They caused us to look for Jesus in the faces and stories of our own people. Because Jesus is there too—at our place and at yours, weaving a narrative of hope that often goes unread.

- If you were going to have 200 people come to your church, who in your congregation would you want to tell their story?
- How can you better notice and tell those stories among your people?
- What difference would that make?

Move with those who are ready to move. It has been said that the only people who like change are babies with dirty diapers. Change is hard. And leading change is particularly hard.

As ministers, we seem to be hard-wired to want everyone to be happy. But waiting for such a moment to occur will paralyze us in our efforts to affect change. Eddie Hammett has often said that you have to "move with the ones who are ready to move." If you can get 20-30 percent of the people on board, you can make a change.

- Is it time for your church to move forward with a particular ministry?
- Are you waiting for 100 percent of your folks to be ready before you move ahead?
- What will it take for you to be able to "move with the ones who are ready to move"?

Note

[1]Dan Southerland, *Transitioning* (Grand Rapids, MI: Zondervan, 1999), 33.

The Journey of Learning to Trust

You've earned chips in the place you work and serve.
There comes a time when you have to spend those chips.

The big decisions aren't always what make or break a congregation. It is the little decisions that have been made along the way that determine how well a church will navigate the big transitions they face.

For a 200-year-old Baptist church where the ministers preached every service in robes, where the strains of a magnificent pipe organ led worship, and where young acolytes lit candles each week, the notion of a service with drums and guitars and contemporary Christian music seemed very out of place, especially in a 140-year-old sanctuary. While it took nearly five years to figure out a way to do it that was "authentically First Baptist," it finally happened.

While many congregations have fallen victim to the so-called "worship wars," FBC found a great unity even with diverse styles of worship. With multiple services, we remained one church. With all the anxiety about such a change, this story, in the end, wasn't really about worship style. It was about trust.

Every five years in my tenure at First Baptist Wilmington presented an opportunity to ask for some honest feedback. As we approached each of these anniversaries, I would choose five members of the church who I thought would be honest and forthright with me and ask them to help me evaluate how I was doing as their pastor. I never wanted to be the last one to know that it was time for me to leave. On my fifth and tenth anniversaries there was an air of enthusiasm for the church that encouraged me to "keep on." But as we approached my fifteenth anniversary, it didn't feel the same. There was nothing wrong particularly, but there was a sameness that seemed to pervade all we were doing. I felt it, and others did, too. It was time for a fresh, new vision at FBC.

It was about this time that we had a staff retreat led by Dr. George Bullard of The Columbia Partnership. Our worship attendance had grown to near 700, so, in preparation for the retreat, George asked us to read a book about the "very large church." In it the author, Lyle Schaller, observed that a lot of churches hit a ceiling when attendance gets to the 700 level. While he couldn't explain the "why" of that phenomenon, he did begin to do research on the churches that were able to break through the 700 level. The basic premise of the book was that "the things that got you to 700 are the very things that will keep you from going past 700." We were stuck, not in a bad way—things were great at our church—but not in a good way either. We had begun to hit this ceiling, and we didn't know how to get past it.

In true facilitator fashion, George did not tell us how to do anything. He did ask us to dream and to imagine what our church might look like in ten years. He called it a "future story" process. Over the course of an afternoon we painted a picture of where we felt God was calling us to lead the church. We discussed virtually every aspect of the church. We filled page after page of newsprint on the walls with dreams—some simple, some practical, some we had never said out loud before. We imagined expanding our footprint in the city for the cause of Christ, filling our pews with folks who looked different from one another, offering multiple worship services for our growing numbers, creating a place of belonging for anyone who walked through our doors. We caught glimpses of a vision of who our church could become. It was energizing.

When we reconvened after supper, George reviewed the long list and then asked us one question: "For First Baptist to look like this in ten years, what has to change?"

"Change?" Jim Everette blurted out, only half in jest. "We have to change?"

But the reality hit us and, in that moment, we suddenly became like small children trying to get up the nerve to jump off the high dive. We were afraid. Truthfully, a lot of things would have to change if the dream that God seemed to be giving us was going to be fully realized.

We began to consider in earnest all the things that had to change. Our role as ministers was probably going to change in some ways, particularly mine. I might not know everyone's name if we continued to grow, and that was scary to me. We were already feeling the pressure. Keeping our arms around the life of the congregation was different at 600 than it was at 400. I knew there were things I would have to let go of. I feared losing the depth of relationships I had built over the years. We feared loss, period.

With each new item on the list, our apprehension grew. A new reality was setting in. We began to identify where the resistance would come from and what it might look and sound like. There was a strong sentiment in the congregation to keep things as they were. People were happy, including with all of us. If it's not broke, why fix it? What if they didn't give a hoot or a holler about some of the changes we were talking about?

When there is a crisis, it is much easier to mobilize folks to change. It is hard to dream a new dream when life is good. Good really is the enemy of great.

We began to count the cost not only in dollars, but also personally and professionally. It was hardly inconsequential this new path we were entering. And fear plays dirty as a conversation partner. It is so much easier to play it safe, in ministry or any place in life. But, as a staff, we had a deep and innate sense that was not what God was calling us to do. God had so much more in mind for First Baptist Church.

We plugged away late into the evening. The task grew more daunting the longer we went.

When it finally appeared that we had exhausted this whole business of change, George asked if there was anything else that needed to change. As we sat there shaking our heads "no," Don Vigus, our long-time minister to youth, spoke up.

"I think there is one more thing that has to change," he said. "I think Mike has to change."

There are "hinge moments" in life: those times when we think we know where we are and where we're headed and, out of the blue, something hinges you in a different direction. This was one of those moments.

The room fell silent, and everyone looked at me. George let the question hang in the air for a moment and then asked if I wanted to hear how and why Don felt I needed to change. Of course, I said "yes." Don explained.

"Mike, I think we all know what God is leading us to do here at First Baptist, but I think you're afraid. You've always been cautious not to do any damage to the church, and that's great; but if this is what God is calling us to do, you are going to have to lead us. We've spent fifteen years building up all these chips (relational capital). What are we saving them for? It's time to spend them."

Don was right. I was afraid. I didn't want to be the pastor who led the church in some way that split the church or harmed the fellowship.

I respected our tradition. I respected all those folks who had invested a lifetime at FBC. Things were going well in the church, and it would have been much easier to go into maintenance mode and not change anything. But we all sensed that this calling was "of God." We had no choice. It was time to spend the chips. What were we saving them for?

Flamingo Road Church

Not knowing exactly what this new calling might look like for us or how we were to live into it, George suggested that I attend a conference on Transitions at the Flamingo Road Church. A couple of months later I did, and I learned a lot about leading change and transition (see the story in the previous chapter). More than that, what I experienced there forever changed my life. There was a passion in the people and a transparency I had not experienced before. There was something spiritual going on that I wanted in the church where I was pastor.

When the conference was over, I left Fort Lauderdale wondering what I would say to the rest of the staff when I got home. There were four ministers on our staff at that time: Don, Jim, Kurt, and me. Driving up the Interstate that afternoon, I couldn't wait until I got home to talk to them. So one by one, I called all three of them. In ways that I couldn't fully explain, I told them that I had been freed up; had lost my fear; had been changed . . . never again to be the same.

As syrupy as that may sound, when I returned to the church, the three of them were eager to hear more details of my Flamingo Road experience. I told them that I didn't think I would ever again feel limited as to what God might do in my life or in our church. I lacked confidence before about being able to lead meaningful change, but my time at FRC helped me to believe I could do it well. I told them I was ready to lead, but I also reminded them that it could be costly—perhaps even to the point of losing our jobs.

People may not want to go where you are burdened to go. Like every church, there were some at our place who didn't want to see change.

I felt led by God into that moment, but, when you read the biblical accounts, sometimes people pay a terrible price for being obedient. It was one thing for me to take risks for myself, but I had a genuine concern for my colleagues and what I might be dragging them into. If any one of them had balked, I think I would have had to find another place to serve. There was no turning back for me now. But all three of them embraced the notion of moving forward, not altogether sure where that might lead us but truly trusting that God would guide us. We had no preconceived plan or agenda. We simply knew that God had called us to be more than we were.

At George Bullard's suggestion and with his guidance, we entered into a second "future story process," this time with twenty-five members of the congregation, to help us to discern what God wanted to do in us and through us. In choosing these lay persons, George challenged us to "not" identify people who simply held office in the church, contending that "elected" folks are not always the ones who are open to change or capable of crafting a new vision. Instead, he said we needed a cadre of folks who were open to, and ready for, what God was doing in the world and who possessed four qualities that George called "readiness factors." We were to look for people who were . . .

1. passionately positive about the church and its future
2. spiritually mature and believing that God was up to something in our midst
3. strategically innovative and ready to risk
4. capable leaders able to inspire and motivate others to be involved in transition and change.

As a staff we identified more than 120 such persons from our congregation as possible members of the future story group. That was incredibly affirming to us. Then came the hard part: paring the list down to just twenty-five. It was not easy. We had to make sure we did not just pick folks who might agree with us or who might support our bias or wishes. We each lobbied for certain people. We sought balance in the group in terms of age and gender and length of time at FBC, but never at the expense of the four readiness factors. In the end, twenty-five names remained on the board, and all but two agreed to serve.

We talk a lot about convergence at FBC; those times when seemingly separate circumstances start moving in the same direction. This is usually a good indication that it is time to pay attention, for the Holy Spirit may very well be at work. Three factors led me to believe that this was one of those times.

First, there was a holy discontent among us. We all realized that while our old church had experienced some significant growth and while things appeared healthy, we were feeling a bit stagnant. Holy discontent makes us restless. It releases our emotional attachments to what is and creates a longing in us for something more.

Second, a change had taken place in me. While the staff and the future story group did not fully understand it, they knew I was at a different place spiritually, and, for the most part, they found that to be exciting.

Third, we were beginning to feel the movement of God's Spirit among us as a future story group. We were listening to each another, thinking outside our comfort zones, and entertaining the notion that there might be more than one way to be church. It was an exciting time. No one wanted to miss a future story meeting.

It was early on in the midst of that process that we identified two young lay women in our church who both became a part of our staff on a part-time basis. The first, Jayne Davis, had begun seminary when we asked her to become our minister of spiritual formation. The second was Jeannie Troutman, whom we asked to become our minister to children.

The very presence of these two women changed the entire dynamic of our staff. Gifted beyond measure and deeply dedicated to the church, both of them began to transform their areas of ministry and, in turn, our staff dynamic. Staff conversations took on a whole new feel, as did those of the future story group. Things were changing more than we knew.

I kept talking about my experience at Flamingo Road, particularly my encounters with the lay people and how their lives had been changed. There was something uniquely formative about that experience, so much so that we decided we needed to go back to FRC, this time as a group, and experience it together—a large and costly proposition. We approached our deacons for funding to send all six staff ministers along with two deacons, Wanda Porter and Carl Williford, both of whom were serving on the future story group. Wanda was the heartbeat of our local mission efforts, and Carl was chair of the diaconate. The fact that the deacons not only approved the funding, but also blessed the whole staff being absent for four days gave indication that our deacons also sensed something new was afoot at First Baptist.

Our group time at FRC proved to be transformative. We had always expected that there was great value in visiting and learning from other churches, but now we had experienced it firsthand. The "Whatever It Takes" attitude of the people at FRC was contagious. Their commitment to a ministry role for every member challenged us to raise the bar for ourselves, and their passion to find ways to share the hope of Christ with those who would never simply just walk through their doors opened our eyes to a different way to think of being church.

Contemporary Worship

When we got back home and processed all we had seen and heard with the future story group, there were many opinions and ideas about what was happening and what needed to happen at First Baptist Church. While a host of issues and opportunities rose to the surface, it was clear that the matter of a new contemporary worship service was emerging as a signature part of our future story. There were simply too many people we would never reach through our traditional worship service.

That we would have a contemporary worship service became a fairly straightforward decision. How we would do it was a far more complicated matter. Multiple questions hung over us. How do you make a change so radically different from what you have always done? Conversations often turned painful as we sought a way to accomplish this major transition without doing damage to the church we all loved so much. For more than four years the staff explored idea after idea.

While on a Lilly grant-funded sabbatical in 2004, my wife and I visited dozens of churches doing contemporary worship. In Ohio we encountered a multi-service mega-church that had a super band with a horn section worthy of some slick Las Vegas show. Then I learned that the leader of the band was indeed "straight from Las Vegas"—complete with a bright red sport coat. In Chicago we heard a band whose leader looked like Jerry Garcia of the Grateful Dead and who, based on his theatrics, apparently thought he was, in fact, Jerry Garcia. In Texas we worshipped with a wonderful Methodist congregation that had a "rented" band. None of them were members of the church, and it was apparent they were just going through the motions to collect a check.

On a visit to a Baptist congregation in Maryland we experienced what felt a bit like what I suppose New Age worship might be. The instrumental band consisted of a guitar, an African drum, and a harp. The music was enchanting and very unlike any church music I had ever experienced. In California we worshipped on a Sunday night in a gym with a thousand candles lit and prayer stations all around. The band was great, and the energy in the room palpable. In North Carolina we worshipped in a brand new sanctuary packed to the corners. The band was okay, but the one lead singer made it seem like a performance—and all about her.

While I am certain that what I saw in all of those churches worked for them, none of it felt like it would work for us. We were stuck, and we knew it. We had come to a place where we felt "called" to offer a worship alternative, but how to do it authentically remained beyond our imagination. Still, we held onto the notion that God would provide a way.

We wrestled a lot with the question of where to offer the contemporary service. Our congregation worships in a sanctuary designed in pre-Civil War 1858. While the sanctuary had been renovated a couple of times (one minor and one significant renovation), it was essentially as it had been for 140 years. We assumed that any changes to the room to accommodate contemporary worship would be met with fierce opposition, so we began to explore some alternative locations.

FBC has a fabulous activities center, complete with a large gym, adjacent meeting rooms, and a nursery area that would have been perfect, but it is located four and a half miles from the downtown campus. If we had used the activities center, we feared that it would divide our Sunday school. With more than 500 participants in Sunday school, we did not want to take that risk. It would have meant two full faculties, which we concluded would have truly constituted a division in the church. Though we knew of multi-location churches, we did not see that as a viable option for FBC at the time.

We then turned our attention to venues close to the downtown campus. We first looked at a nearby gym and an auditorium owned by the Catholic church, but multiple issues made it unworkable. We explored space in the historic city hall building down the street, but that also had too many obstacles to be a satisfactory space.

In the end we came to believe that we needed to have the service in our sanctuary, the place where we had always worshipped. But none of us had any sense of how we might do it in a manner that would be acceptable to the church. We feared the push back and had no idea how to handle it.

After much prayer and discussion we determined to launch the contemporary service in our sanctuary, and we decided to do it on Sunday mornings at 9 o'clock before Sunday school. At the time we were doing two traditional services. The earlier one had no choir, but that was the only real difference. We sang the same hymns, read the same litanies, and observed all the same rituals and special observances in both services. We promised that our 11 a.m. traditional service would remain unchanged, complete with robes, candles, and a chancel choir. But the early service would become very different.

As if the addition of a contemporary service was not enough "change" to handle, we were on a roll and had more to our vision for worship that we wanted to put in place. We made plans for a third service we called Vintage, to be held at 8 a.m. in our chapel. It was to be a more contemplative service where Communion was served each Sunday. We had many members who had come from other faith traditions who longed for weekly Communion. We also wanted to create a worship environment that was drastically different from the high-energy contemporary service and the much more formal traditional service—a more intimate setting that sought God in prayerful stillness.

We launched the Vintage service at the same time as the contemporary service, but we kept it for only two years. Attendance dwindled from fifty or so at the beginning down to just a handful. Not all visions turn out the way you hope they will. New initiatives take more time, energy, creativity, and resources than we realize sometimes—and there was just not enough to go around. We shortchanged the Vintage service. We did not give it our best. Without someone to nurture the service and give it the care and attention it needed, it withered on the vine. The contemporary service, which we called "The Journey," commanded all of our attention.

While there was some grumbling about our plan to launch a contemporary worship service, mostly from the people who liked the early traditional service, the push back was far less than we had expected. We communicated every detail of the plan to the congregation by every means possible. We answered every question as honestly as we knew how to do.

But perhaps Don Vigus had been right. We had built up a lot of chips, and now we were spending them. In retrospect, we came to believe that our people simply trusted us—both the staff and the future story group. That is a wonderful discovery to make, and one that can come only when you step out in faith and begin to take a few risks.

Unexpected Provision

With the "where" of the service having been settled, we now had to focus on the "how." Kurt Wachtel, our minister of music and worship, began the daunting task of pulling together a band. We were committed to excellence, and there just didn't seem to be a lot of rock musician potential in our historic downtown mix of folks. But when God gives you a vision, he gives you the resources to accomplish it—if you are willing to look in some unexpected places to find them.

Someone heard one of our deacons talking with a friend about "getting the band back together." When Kurt approached him, it turned out that he was just joking, that he had never had a band. But he did play a little guitar. Another member, who is a plumbing contractor, joined in the practices. A percussionist, who is a Christian counselor, played bongos, congas, and a few other things that made "fun sounds." A bass player emerged along with a couple of keyboard players. Each one of them was a member of the church, and each was an amateur. The only professionals were Kurt and his wife, Jean, both of whom played keyboards. But we still needed a drummer.

Kurt had been searching for a drummer since rehearsals began in early February. He had exhausted virtually every resource, lead, and contact he knew. Desperation was setting in for this integral part of the band.

One Sunday morning as I was standing at the door greeting people as they left the service, I recognized the son of a couple in the church who I knew to be a drummer in a quasi-Christian rock band. I didn't know him well, but I briefly explained our situation to him to see if he might have any interest or, at the least, a suggestion. He was very gracious but explained that he and his band were on the road most every weekend and were often touring in Europe and Asia. He wasn't available to make that kind of commitment.

"But," he said, "you had one of the best drummers in the southeast worshipping with you today, Buddy Bryan."

I was flabbergasted. While Buddy and his wife were members, they only worshipped with us sporadically and I didn't know them well. I never knew or imagined that Buddy was a drummer.

On Monday morning I told Kurt about the conversation. We had no home phone number for Buddy, but Jim Everette went to work and obtained his cell number. That Tuesday, Kurt got hold of Buddy—in Los Angeles of all places. He was out there laying down the drum tracks for an upcoming CD. Kurt explained to him what we were starting and that we were in desperate need of a drummer. Without hesitation, Buddy was on board. Eight years later, Buddy is still our primary drummer.

Despite this incredible addition to the band, the amateurs still outnumbered the professionals. I'll never forget stopping by one of their early rehearsals in the choir room. They all sat arrayed in a circle with each guitar paired to small amps scattered about the room. It has to be said: They were bad—far worse than any of the other bands I had heard on my sabbatical! Perhaps we weren't specific enough in our prayers for musicians.

The next day I expressed my concerns to Kurt. He reminded me that it takes time to put a band together, especially when most of them had not been playing for years. It was a call for patience. I was worried, but I trusted Kurt.

Musicians were not our only concern. There was also the technical side of this whole endeavor. The architectural constraints of our Gothic chancel precluded installing "drop down" screens needed to project song lyrics, sermon points, videos, graphics, and all of the other creative worship elements we imagined generating. We tossed out and summarily rejected idea after idea until one day Kurt burst into my office.

"I know what to do about the screens. We can cut two holes in the front wall . . ."

I stopped him before he could say another word.

"We will not cut holes in the wall of this 140-year-old sanctuary!" I thought he had lost his mind.

Kurt pressed on with his explanation. We would cut two large holes on either side of the chancel, place two 65" LCD TVs in the holes, and then put a frame around them and cover them with quarter-inch painted plywood that would be held in place with Velcro.

It was now official. The process had robbed Kurt of his senses.

One of our deacons, a building contractor, convinced me we could do it just as Kurt said and that no one would ever know. That old fear began to creep back into my soul as I imagined gaping holes in both walls flanking either side of the pulpit as folks came in for worship one Sunday morning. You can't undo something like that! Why couldn't this be easy?

In point of fact, the screens were put into place and covered for "months" before most people in the traditional service even knew they were there.

Kurt began to put together a list of the sound and video equipment we would need to do the service well. We obtained price quotes and began to inch toward our May launch of the new service and schedule. Calling the service "The Journey" truly captured our sense of this pathway of faith we were on and were hoping to call others to. The band was aptly called "deepwater" as they were leading us to places we had never been before as a congregation. In those early days I would have said it was because we were in over our heads!

It was time to get our people ready. We talked about the launch of the new worship schedule each week with great excitement. We prepared a special newsletter that explained the nature of the three services, reminding people that while other elements might be different in each service, the sermon or message would be the same.

Two weeks before our launch date the equipment package arrived. Late on that Saturday night Kurt called me with the good news that everything had been installed and all the portable equipment worked as it should. This was clearly an answer to prayer.

Just a few hours later, at 6:30 the next morning, as I was getting ready for church, Kurt called me again.

"We can't do this next Sunday!" he blurted out without so much as a "Hello."

I calmly asked what had changed between 9 o'clock the night before and this morning. Kurt said he had been awake most of the night confronting what now had become obvious to him. The "set up" and "take down" time required each week simply would not work. We often had weddings on Saturdays that would require set-up on Sunday morning before the band could practice at 7:45 a.m. The take-down could not be completed in time to allow pre-service practice for the choir at the 11 a.m. service. Kurt insisted that we needed to make it a permanent installation of sound and video equipment for the contemporary service to work in the old sanctuary.

We were both distraught. He apologized over and over again. I told him that as disappointed as I was—and that the congregation would be—I trusted him. The truth is that we had decided to go the "portable" route to save money, but it simply proved impractical in our 1860s sanctuary with all of its physical constraints.

At the close of both worship services that Sunday I informed the congregation of our dilemma. I apologized through my unexpected tears. All the build-up, all the anticipation, all the hard work seemed for naught. I could not tell them when we would be ready to launch The Journey or how much more it might cost. Talk about a "down" day at FBC. This was it. The "anti" crowd began to whisper. Then God surprised us yet again.

On Monday morning I received a call from one of our older members who was not in favor of the contemporary service. He asked how much it was going to cost to make the equipment installation permanent. I told him that we would have to get the engineers back and get a bid for going beneath the floor and installing all the cable and such. He said he wanted to know how much it was going to cost before we did anything. I could only imagine how he would use that information to thwart our effort. It was looking like a long summer ahead.

Finally, in early July we got the quote: $70,000 more. Before we took it to our church leadership, I called the man who had called back in May. I swallowed hard as I told him the amount we needed.

He said, "Tell Marie (our financial secretary) I will have a check to her for the full amount this afternoon."

Stunned by his most gracious offer, I reminded him that he had not been in favor of the whole project from the start.

"You are right," he said. "But I believe you boys believe this is what God would have you do for our church, and I want to help you make it happen."

To this day, this man has never worshipped in The Journey service, but God used him in a powerful way to make that service happen.

Multiple Services, One Church

On a bright September Sunday, The Journey began. At 8:45 a.m. the room was packed, the energy was amazing, and the band was really good. The four-month delay had allowed them to hone their skills and create a sound that fit us perfectly. The band simply rocked!

In our tradition we give an "invitation" at the end of each service, usually for church membership or baptism. At the end of the first Journey service, one of our deacons who had been a life-long member at FBC came down to the front from his back-row seat in the balcony. He asked if he could speak to the congregation. While highly unusual, but because I fully trusted him, I encouraged him to speak. It was a moment I'll never forget.

Deak Walden began by noting how he had been a member of FBC his entire life and also how he had been opposed to The Journey service from the beginning. Then he said that he had never experienced anything like that day's worship and that he had never been more proud of FBC than he was that Sunday. He thanked everyone for being the kind of church that could create a place for everybody. It was a defining moment for all of us.

Three years later, worship attendance averaged 840 in the two services—divided virtually equally between the two.

It takes an amazingly gifted minister of music to birth a dream like this at a place like ours, and FBC is blessed beyond measure. Trained in traditional sacred music, Kurt Wachtel was at home in a tux with a baton in hand directing an orchestra and choir at Christmas or Easter. One person who played with the local symphony asked of me, "Where did you find this guy? We are not accustomed to church musicians with his level of talent." Kurt knew and did fine music.

Yet when we began to talk about the praise team and the extra night of practice it would require, Kurt accepted all of that with no questions. To have a couple like Kurt and Jean, our organist, so committed and talented that they could and would lead the music in two such diverse services is simply a gift from God. Not all music people can or want to do that. Kurt had assured our folks all along that whatever we did in The Journey it would be "authentically First Baptist." He delivered in full on that promise.

With the two services on either side of our Sunday school, it allowed us to remain "one" church. With most folks in The Journey service dressing much more casually and those in the traditional service in coats and ties, we found that our Sunday school covered the whole fashion spectrum. From day one there was hardly a complaint. While the two services were dramatically different from one another, no one in our church would say that we had created two churches or a divided congregation. That would have been too high a price to pay.

When people have asked which service I like the best, my standard answer has always been "yes." They are both wonderful. Every Sunday while I was still the pastor, I got to sing the grand old hymns of the faith and participate in the rituals that had defined us for generations . . . the *Gloria Patri*, the Doxology, the Lord's Prayer. An excellent chancel choir and organist offered a weekly anthem that always seemed to stir my soul. Each and all of those components remain an essential part of our traditional worship.

The Journey is everything the traditional service isn't. Typically, the music is high energy with a dozen or so singers flanking the band. The passion of the band and singers radiates in their faces and voices and playing. For Communion, everyone comes to the front to be served as they hear the words, "The body of Christ broken for you," "The blood of Christ shed for you." It is a more personal experience as those words are spoken by deacons offering the Communion elements to each person who comes forward. It is an awesome experience that really does feel just like First Baptist.

While few people would describe us as cutting edge, The Journey service has opened up a whole new aspect of worship planning to us, giving us a freedom to experiment with different elements in worship. From the use of *Everybody Loves Raymond* clips for a series on family, to the band playing Kool & the Gang's "Celebration" on a baptism Sunday, to prayer requests being offered on bright colorful Post-It notes and placed on brown butcher block paper that lined the walls of the sanctuary, we have been stretched in our creativity in communicating God's message with relevance and cultivating an environment where worship happens. The old limitations have passed away.

While there were a few nay-sayers along the way, the one I had to hear from the most was my wife. A member of the chancel choir, she begged me not to pursue the new contemporary service. My assurances that we would do it differently from the other places we had visited proved unconvincing. But a month after our launch of The Journey, she said, "If I could only worship in one service, it would be The Journey." She was not the only one.

Cultivating Hopeful Imagination

Pay attention to the Spirit. As you read this story, what did the Spirit prompt in you regarding your own congregation and context?

• Whispers: How is God stirring up your imagination?
• Groans: What needs in your church or community do you think about?
• Praises: What resources or individuals or opportunities come to mind?

Earn trust and spend your chips wisely. Mike often says that every minister is given a certain amount of trust when you come to a church; the rest you have to earn. We think about trust in the big moments—the difficult decisions, the crises—but trust is earned in little ways every day and builds up over time . . . when you show up at the hospital, when you return phone calls and emails, when you keep your word . . . no matter how small. The things we can mistakenly dismiss sometimes as being unimportant or inconsequential are, in fact, the things that lay the foundation from which the big dreams are launched.

At our place we call it "earning chips." It's all about building relationships and being trustworthy. It is what gives folks confidence to follow you when the road gets a little rocky or when it becomes difficult to see where the path ahead is leading. They have come to know your care as genuine and your word to be true. You have been responsible in the little things, and so they are more apt to trust you in the big ones.

There are times when we need to spend those chips. Launching The Journey service was one of those moments for us. It was a time when, as leaders, we had to push the chips we had earned through the years to the middle of the table and ask our folks, "Will you be 'all in' with us?"

If we never feel a need to spend our chips, if the plans before us rarely entail much risk, it is unlikely that we are seeking much of a vision from God.

• How attentive are you to the small, relational details of ministry?
• Is there a vision before you worth spending your chips on?
• Do you have enough chips to move forward, or do you need to wait and earn more of a right to ask folks to take the risk of following you?

Trust one another. I can still remember where I was when I got the call from Mike that the plug had temporarily been pulled on the launch of The Journey service. It was about 7:30 a.m. and I was in my car turning off Market Street onto Martin Luther King Parkway, on my way to the church for worship. It was a shocking moment seared in my mind. Everything we had been doing for the last several months was focused on that launch, just one week away—everything. It would be a high-profile setback, and could open the door a crack for those who had their doubts about a contemporary service.

I didn't understand a lot of the details of the explanation of the sound and video installation. All I needed to hear I heard in one phrase: "Kurt says we're not ready." I was dumbfounded and incredibly disappointed. I was worried about how this might sidetrack the ultimate launch of the service. But I trusted Kurt Wachtel completely, and simply said, "Okay."

Trust is a fundamental characteristic of our staff. We are all passionate about what we do, but we know that ultimately it's not about us. We pursue excellence in our areas of ministry, but we are never in competition with one another. We can speak very honestly and openly with each other as we talk through the issues and challenges of ministry. I know that I am free to be myself in staff conversations; to say what I think and not wonder if I'm going to pay for it later.

We can disagree greatly about how to handle a particular situation —and we do at times—but when we leave the room, we stand together. It becomes our decision. We are all in. No one undermines a decision they don't like. No one tells folks in the congregation, "I never wanted us to do that . . ." There are no divisions or alliances.

You will never hear a staff member speaking badly about another staff member to members of the congregation—ever. The congregation realizes this. They comment on it. They value that. Our trust of one another creates a safe environment in which to live and worship together, and it develops trust in the congregation.

Such trust also gives us an identity as a staff. When we are about to respond in a way that is more driven by emotion or pride, there is always a voice from among the group that reminds us "That's not who we are" or when the right way is the hard way, the voice that says "Because this is who we are."

- Who are you as a staff?
- What is your identity as a staff?
- Are your staff relationships healthy?
- Is your staff situation tough right now?
- How can you improve your staff relationships?
- What kind of environment does your staff dynamic create for your congregation?
- Does your staff dynamic give the congregation a safe and solid place from which to take risks for God?

Identify passionately positive people. As we sought to discern God's vision for our church, George Bullard challenged us to identify people in the congregation who were open to, and ready for, what God was doing in the world and who possessed four "readiness factors" (see page 49).

The fact that we could identify more than 120 people in our congregation who fit that profile gave us great encouragement and courage as we looked to the future. God hadn't shown us where we were going yet, but he reminded us who was going with us—incredible, committed, capable folks.

- As you think about George Bullard's "readiness factors" and the people in your congregation, what names come to mind?
- How does it feel to think about moving into the future together with these people?
- What first step might you take with them on this journey?

Never write off your critics. Who could ever imagine that someone so opposed to the launch of a contemporary worship service would be the person to give the large financial gift that made the service possible?

Who could ever imagine someone opposed to the contemporary service coming down to the front of the sanctuary at the conclusion of the first service and offering a word of blessing and affirmation to the congregation for becoming the kind of church that could create a place for everyone?

Only God can create that kind of poetry.

The two gentlemen in this story are long-time, well-respected members of First Baptist Church. Their opinions mean a lot and carry a lot of weight. And their opposition to the contemporary worship service was born out of the same love for FBC that those who championed the service shared.

It is not easy to move forward when everyone is not on board, but it is critical not to marginalize those who don't share the vision. For one, they keep us honest. They help us make better decisions. You think more fully about things when you know you may be called to explain yourself. And secondly, you never know when and how God may use them to move his vision forward.

- Who are the thoughtful critics among you?
- How are you engaging them as you discern God's dream for your church?

Dream a new dream. When there is a crisis, it is much easier to mobilize folks to change. It is hard to dream a new dream when life is good. Good really is the enemy of great.

Don't wait until the wheels have come off of the bus to dream a new dream. Do it while you are healthy. Resist the lull of the status quo.

- In what ways is good the enemy of great in your congregation?
- What would great look like?
- What would have to happen to move you from good to great?

Making "Yes" the Default Setting

Look for ways to make things happen,
not barriers to keep things from happening.
Involve as many people as possible in the planning process,
even and especially your critics.

Too often, churches get stuck in a pattern of making "why we can't do something" their first reaction to opportunities. Making "yes" the default setting for your congregation doesn't happen overnight. As with forming any new habit, it requires time, intentionality, and self-management.

We don't realize how many times our first response is "no" until we commit to saying "yes." But if our congregational life in Christ is to be characterized by a resounding "yes" to God, it has to begin in the big and small decisions we make as a church each and every day.

When I became pastor of First Baptist Wilmington, it made little difference who came up with the idea or dream or ministry or even, really, how good it was. There was always someone ready to say no. Some of that negativity was driven by reality. We didn't have a lot of money in those early days, nor did we have much imagination. Even the members of the search committee that called me described their vision for the church as "at least staying where we are."

The notion of growth and evangelism scared the committee members. They had visions of manipulative preaching and extended altar calls at the very mention of the word evangelism. I had a very different view of ways to share the gospel and told them that if they didn't want to grow as a church, both spiritually and numerically, they shouldn't call me. That began a wonderful conversation about growth and a redemptive and godly way to go about it.

To say that I was in over my head does not begin to capture the reality of those earliest days.

The congregation didn't know how to welcome my wife and me—so mostly they did not. In point of fact, during my third week at the church one member, as she was leaving the financial secretary's office, stuck her head in my door and said, "Dr. Queen, I guess I should say to your face what I have said behind your back. Since you have come to the church, you have destroyed our ability to worship God. But Dr. Queen, I was here when you got here and I'll be here when you are gone."

I suppose that was her way of saying, "Welcome to Wilmington."

I was very inexperienced as a preacher, so my preaching proved to be a bit of a struggle in those early years. One of my best friends in the church told me some years ago that he and his wife almost left the church when I came to be the pastor because, as he said, "I thought you were the worst preacher I had ever heard."

My preaching was bad; I knew it. I was working on my new craft, but that would take time. I knew we needed some kind of success, somewhere, as I grew into the preaching role.

One of my mentors, the late Dr. Chevis Horne, cautioned me that there are some things you should not attempt in a church until you have earned the right to do so. Thus, I set about earning that right—earning my chips, so to speak. None of it was all that glamorous, but all of it was foundational to everything else that followed.

I had to learn to settle for small, achievable victories in the beginning. Not a lot of memorable work took place in the first five years, but a few decisions, I believe, proved significant.

First, I began my ministry at FBC by visiting every member of the church who was confined to a nursing home or their home. When asked by the deacons why that was such a high first priority, I told them that as anxious as they were about me as their new pastor, the shut-ins were even more anxious. They imagined that the new preacher might be called upon to do their funeral, and they worried that I wouldn't know them. As word spread that I had made visits to those good saints of the church, some barriers began to get lowered. That single decision did more to anchor my ministry at First Baptist than anything else I did in the first five years.

Second, we began a renewal of our youth and children's music ministry. Three months before my call, Jeff Lewis had come to FBC as minister of music. He was a superbly gifted organist/choirmaster. We both hit the ground running. Jeff talked someone into buying a full set of hand bells, and another kind soul into buying hand chimes for the children. He began recruiting youth, children, and adults for those new bell choirs. He also began to develop youth and children's choirs. The adult chancel choir was about all that he had inherited.

Early that fall, Jeff asked me if I had ever done a "hanging of the greens" service for Advent. I was familiar with it because the church my wife and I attended during my seminary days had conducted such a service. We began to kick around the notion of doing one at FBC on the first Sunday night of Advent. Immediately, the no's began. One staff member was certain that no one would come to a service at night downtown in the winter darkness. While it was true that we were only fifteen years removed from the race riots of the early 1970s, we felt that people would come out for this event. We pressed ahead with the idea.

The next hurdle was money. We didn't need a lot, but finances were tight. In my second finance committee meeting in September of that first year, the chair called for a cut in the budget for the next year. His rationale was solid, as he said, "We won't make budget this year, and we have a 'rookie' preacher." That meeting went on for a long time with me, the rookie preacher, begging these church leaders not to take a step backward. In the end, I won. We raised the budget from 1986 to 1987 by $72. That is not a typo. $72! Of course, the chairman was correct. We did not make the budget that year or the next or the next. But somehow we found a few hundred dollars to buy the greenery and the candles for the Advent service.

As word began to spread about the "hanging of the greens," people began asking questions about it. When someone inquired, we gave them something to do in the service. Every Sunday school class had some part in hanging the greens or decorating the platform with poinsettias. Some ladies in the church undertook making the chrismon ornaments to decorate the tree in the sanctuary. (Some of those ornaments are still in use at FBC today, thirty years later.)

I told Jeff that we needed every music group to have some part in the service. We were going to do all we could to have as many people as possible participating, in the hopes that they would bring their family with them. Back in those days our average worship attendance was around 375.

To say that Jeff and I were a bit anxious did not quite capture our emotions. This needed to go well. We prayed that it would. Earlier that Sunday afternoon we rehearsed with everyone so they would know what to do and when to do it in the service. People began to arrive early. They brought friends and family with them. The room began to fill— downstairs, the balcony. And then the ushers went into Sunday school classrooms, dragging folding chairs into every nook and cranny of the sanctuary. It was standing room only!

All I did that evening was offer a welcome and a Christmas blessing at the end. As people filed out, there were hugs and words of appreciation from every soul. Jeff was overwhelmed at the positive comments he received. The music was great, and the old church house was alive with the greenery and the candles and the colors.

One of the last persons to leave the sanctuary that evening was Dr. Bertram Williams Jr. Bert is a tall man, a surgeon and a farmer with a no-nonsense demeanor. With his wife Ellen, Bert stopped at the door.

"Mike," he said, "I have only one real regret about this night." I nodded, trying to get myself ready for his critique. "I only wish my mother had lived long enough to see us have to put out folding chairs in old First Baptist Church."

Bert shook my hand and moved out into the night.

When I finally got back into the sanctuary, the only person left was Jeff. He was physically and emotionally drained. I asked him if he knew what had happened that night. I told him that he had become the minister of music and that I had become the pastor. People needed something good to happen, and the hanging of the greens proved to be that catalyst for us. If we could pull that off, what else might we be able to do?

While not nearly as dramatic as some of the other stories of our congregation, the transformation that took place that night allowed us to find ways to say yes to new ideas and ministries that were truly remarkable. There was no one event that made it so, but over time, our mindset shifted.

It is easy to think of all the reasons not to do something. There are risk factors, cost concerns, lack of leadership, and a host of other roadblocks to overcome, but slowly that kind of ingrained thinking can give way to a new way of being church—as it did in Wilmington.

While no single event generated this change, one decision did. With great intentionality, we consistently involved as many people in the decision-making process as was practical and possible. People began to take ownership of the church and its ministries. Running ideas by multiple groups of people and operating with as much transparency as we could, people began to trust. They trusted the staff, the committees, and each other. It was a beautiful thing to see.

Of course, it did not always go as smoothly as we might have liked, but we accomplished a lot of things. We found new ways to say yes and, over time, felt an increasing freedom to try new things—almost any new thing.

As one member said a few years back, "The thing I like most about our church is that we can try anything and not worry about whether it is a success or not."

That was a new way of being church for us.

Openness and Transparency

Friends often ask about our structure at FBC. It is a fairly normal kind of governance model with deacons and committees. But the difference at FBC is that we let committees do their work. Everything does not require diaconate approval. The really big things do, but for the most part the committees are autonomous. There are a handful of times when something needs congregational approval. When people ask how we knew what required approval and what did not, my answer was always, "We just know." It really came down to a matter of trust and common sense.

In my fifth year as pastor at FBC, it became clear that there was some much-needed work on the physical plant. By then the sanctuary was 125 years old, and little had changed over that time. Certainly lighting and heating and air conditioning had been added, but that was about all. One of the pitfalls of such a great old room is that it was designed by a Philadelphia architect for how church was done in 1858.

The predominant architectural feature of the sanctuary was a Gothic arch that curved above the pulpit. Halfway up the arch and above the pulpit was a platform that had held the old organ. Over time it also provided space for a "paid quartet" of singers that later expanded to a "double paid quartet." When the church moved to a volunteer choir in the 1920s, renovation of that space yielded room for twenty-seven choir members—and not a single person more. To complicate matters, when the twenty-seventh person entered the choir loft, he or she had to close the door after entering and then unfold a chair in which to sit. That blocked door was the only way in and out of the loft, unless, of course, one was willing to jump over the railing and down to the main floor.

Modern building codes would have never allowed such a structure to be built.

We secured the services of ADW Architects of Charlotte, North Carolina to advise us as to how to solve our problem. We were beginning to grow. We needed more choir space. We needed a larger platform area. But those needs were nothing compared to the desire to keep the sanctuary exactly as it was. While we knew there would be resistance to renovation, we clearly underestimated the intensity of that reality.

Mike Dyer of ADW did a fabulous job of listening to input from everyone who wanted to have a say in the matter. Over the course of several meetings he heard it all. He told me more than once that he could help us discover a palatable solution to our problem. He said, "What we will seek to do is make the changes in the same way Samuel Sloan (the Philadelphia architect) might have done them if he was designing the sanctuary for how you do church today."

While many of us were skeptical of his claims, Mike was our only option. When he finally came back with a plan, he also brought an artist's rendering of what it would look like. The committee was amazed at how he had retained the arch motif and of really how little it would change visually. The choir was brought down to the platform with space for sixty-plus voices. The pulpit was pulled forward and the platform expanded. That cost us a couple of rows of pews on the front and the side—"Amen pews" that were never used. The baptistery was moved up above all of that and centered under a wooden cross in the main Gothic arch. It was a stunningly beautiful picture.

With enthusiasm, the plan was presented to the diaconate and adopted unanimously. Then we mailed to each family unit in the church a brochure with the rendering, cost estimates, and list of other items to be included in the overall project. A couple of church-wide informational sessions/discussions followed. Not everyone was happy with the plan.

A vote was set during a "called" Sunday afternoon church business conference held in the very sanctuary that was the subject of the debate. In our congregation, the pastor serves as "moderator" of all church-wide meetings. A crowd of 250 or so folks gathered that day to vote. The motion was made and seconded to proceed with the project. Then there was time for questions and comments. After two and a half hours of spirited debate and banter, someone finally "called the previous question." The body voted to cut off debate and vote on the measure.

It proved to be the toughest moment in my twenty-five years as moderator. The vote, done by raised hands, was two to one in favor of the plan. What that meant was that seventy or eighty people had voted against it. We closed in prayer and began to make our way out of the building. It was my sense that most of us left that day exhausted and drained from the process. Heated words had been spoken. People had to be asked to wait their turn to speak. It was intense. A few leaders came by to offer congratulations, but it didn't feel like we had won much of anything. With that level of opposition, could we even think about moving forward?

The next morning I received a call from one of our men who was a deacon emeritus. He asked if he could come see me. Thirty minutes later he stood in my office.

"Mike," he said, "I know you know that I am intensely opposed to what you are trying to do to our church. I have no intention of giving one penny to fund this foolish proposal. (So far as I know, he never did.) But I want you to know that I thought yesterday's meeting was the finest one I have ever been privileged to attend at First Baptist. Everyone's voice, including my own, was heard, and the body made a decision. That is as it should be. Thank you for the transparency and openness of the process."

He turned and left my office. I followed him to the front door and thanked him for his kind words.

Not everyone was happy. They never are. As a matter of fact, we fell short in our capital campaign to raise the funds for that sanctuary renovation.

But the level of openness and transparency that characterized the process, the widening of the circle by giving an opportunity for every voice to be heard, became, from that point on, a hallmark of how things would be done at FBC. Such a process always takes longer. It is always messier. But over time, people began to know that the process—and other people, staff, and laity—could be trusted. There was not some small group who "ran the church," as sometimes had been charged. We were in this together. We were getting ready for our future, and we didn't even know it.

In the late 1990s it became evident that we would need to make a decision about denominational affiliation. Members of First Baptist Church had been present in Augusta, Georgia in 1845 when the Southern Baptist Convention (SBC) was formed. The Convention held its annual meeting in our church in the late 1880s. It would not be an easy divorce after 155 years of marriage. Feelings ran strong and deep. But it had become a matter of integrity for us. Women had long held the office of deacon, and we had female ministers on staff. Since the SBC had taken a rather pronounced stand in opposition to such practices, we needed to express our true identity.

A study team of twenty-five persons—note the large size of the group—led by the son of life-long SBC missionaries, met for more than a year and conducted dozens of informational meetings and listening sessions. You don't make decisions like that behind closed doors. Transparency is vital to the process, and it builds trust. In the end the study team recommended that we no longer identify our church as Southern Baptist. Our gym was packed that night as we prepared to make this historic decision. The vote was not unanimous. It was 275 to 2.

A couple of families left the church as a result of the decision. But it was the correct decision for us. Some members criticized us for taking so long, but taking our time and making sure that others were "on board" made all the difference. Timing is everything.

Bringing Others on Board

Back in the '90s, when we were launching our second capital campaign, our consultant told us that someone from the church would have to give more than $200,000 if we were to achieve our goal. I told him that was impossible. Such a person or family did not exist in our congregation.

A few days later, one of our deacons walked into the church office in his work clothes and boots and asked to speak to me. He told me that he and his wife had prayed about it and were prepared to make the $200,000-plus pledge we needed to insure the campaign's success. My jaw dropped. I could hardly believe it.

He asked me if I knew how much he and his wife had pledged to the first capital campaign to renovate the sanctuary five years earlier. I told him that I didn't know what anyone gave, other than my wife and me. He told me that they had pledged and given one dollar. My jaw dropped again.

They had assumed that I was just the new preacher trying to make a name for myself and that I was, in turn, going to leave their church in my dust as I moved on to another place.

"We were wrong," he said. "We never dreamed our church could be what it is today. We did nothing the last time, so we want to make up for it this time."

Trust takes time to build.

In that second campaign, we raised a million dollars more than our goal. Timing—God's timing—is everything. It was worth the wait— a long obedience in the same direction.

Cultivating Hopeful Imagination

Pay attention to the Spirit. As you read this story, what did the Spirit prompt in you regarding your own congregation and context?

• Whispers: How is God stirring up your imagination?
• Groans: What needs in your church or community do you think about?
• Praises: What resources or individuals or opportunities come to mind?

Start with saying "Yes." We think of saying yes or no as a particular response to a specific situation. Of course, in many ways that is true.

But more than we realize, saying yes or no is an ingrained way of thinking. We are wired for one way or another. It's not that we always and only say one or the other. But when an opportunity arises, we discover that we are either wired for yes—and immediately look for ways to make it happen—or we are wired for no—and quickly create hoops to be jumped through and obstacles to be overcome, daring to be convinced that yes could ever be a possibility.

The truth is, we don't realize how often we say no until we commit to saying yes. It is true for individuals, and it is true for congregations.

God doesn't ask us to do more than we can do or to give what we don't have. But when we develop the habit of starting with yes, we discover that we are capable of far more than we ever thought possible. And we begin to see the resources we hold and the world around us in a very different way.

It's not that we never say no at FBC. We simply start with yes. We look for ways to make it happen.

- What is the default setting for your congregation: "Yes" or "No"?
- When opportunities come your way, is your first inclination to look for ways to make them happen or to list the reasons why they cannot work?
- What does your pattern of saying yes or no indicate about your openness to what God wants to do in your midst? About how you see the world and your congregation's role in it? About the resources you hold?
- Where in your current decision making could you practice saying yes?

Widen the circle. Over the years, how we have gone about the work of planning and decision making has become as highly valued as the plans and the decisions we have made.

While ideas may begin in a core of staff or lay leaders, the push is always to widen the circle of the conversation. Whether it is giving folks something to do in the hanging of the greens service to encourage ownership of the idea or letting every voice be heard in the decision to renovate the sanctuary, involving the largest number of people in the process as is possible and practical has served us well in building a deep and abiding trust in the congregation that is rooted in openness, involvement, and transparency.

- How do you go about making big decisions as a congregation?
- Is it the perception in your church that a small group of people makes all the decisions or that every voice is important?
- How can you widen the circle of conversation and engagement?

Taking on Tradition

When you start following God's purpose, God will start making ways.

Sacred cows are alive and well in congregational life. If we are going to move into the future that God has for our churches, we have to learn to hold those traditions with an open hand—not a clenched fist—ready and willing to let them go if opportunities with more kingdom value present themselves. Most traditions are not bad. If they were, it would be easy to let go of them. What is difficult is letting go of something good in order to make room for something great.

Every time a vacancy occurred on our staff at First Baptist Wilmington, rather than simply filling that slot, we took time to evaluate where our ministry was and what we needed then. Such was the case when our full-time minister of education for adults and children left to plant a new church in another city. Jim Everette and I decided that we needed someone to fill the children's position and another person to coordinate adult education. We created two part-time positions and began looking within the church family to find the right people for the jobs. Jeannie Troutman and Jayne Davis were right in every way.

Children's Ministry

When looking for someone to lead children's ministry, I told Jim that I thought we needed a "momma." We agreed to ask Jeannie to be our part-time minister to children on an "interim" basis. We had been accustomed to a full-time seminary-trained person in that role, but somehow it did not feel like a step back to call a mother with no formal theological training. In fact, it has proven to be a huge step forward for children's ministry at FBC.

When I called Jeannie to explore her interest in such a position, I was greeted by crying on the other end of the phone. She explained how she and her husband Jeff had been praying about a lot of things in their lives. She was feeling a pull to work with children. She was unsure of her place at FBC. That summer she had participated in the Henry Blackaby course, *Experiencing God.* There was one line from that study that changed her entire outlook at FBC: "God is working in your church," Blackaby wrote. "Your job is to figure out where and join him in that work."

Jeannie began to pray: "God, you know I'm not happy here. Show me where you are working in this place. Help me to make a difference. Change me or change this church." Then came my phone call. But with that call and Jeannie's tears came a lot of questions. She and I agreed to meet and talk through her concerns. They were many.

Some folks in the church didn't like it that the minister to children position had been reduced to part time. Others thought we needed someone with more training. Jeannie asked about those issues and a whole lot more. Finally, I told her that, while the position was interim, my hope was that someday it would become permanent and full time.

As she prepared to accept the position, Jeannie asked, "What do you want me to do?" I told her I wanted her to make it her ministry; to create a model in which she wanted her own son to learn about what it means to be a follower of Jesus. I wanted her fingerprints all over the children's ministry of FBC. Today they are. Her passion for faith development in children and her ability to bring together creative and dedicated workers are nothing short of amazing.

The sheer joy and enthusiasm of the children point to their love of Jesus and to their love of serving others in Christ's name. From upbeat music to hands-on mission projects to caring for people on the other side of the world, the children at FBC are learning a way of discipleship that we believe will be with them for life.

The first thing Jeannie did was to recruit people to serve on the children's ministry committee who were committed to, and willing to be a part of, setting a new course. What unfolded in children's ministry at FBC may not be right for every church, but it was right for us at the time we did it. Taking on the sacred cows of "the way we have always done things" in children's ministry took a lot of courage on Jeannie's part. A fair number of very good people did not approve of the new direction. A few disengaged. But the end result has been a children's ministry that is at the very heart of all we are about at FBC.

The first sacred cow on the menu was Vacation Bible School. VBS was stagnant. We typically had seventy children participating, ages three to sixth grade, with only a handful of visitors in the mix. The truth is no one wanted to invite their friends. As one mother confessed, "I have a hard time getting my own child to go." There was nothing wrong with what we were doing; it just wasn't exciting the kids. We struggled to staff VBS. Most of our volunteers were the mothers of the children participating. Programmatically, it was particularly difficult to keep the three-year-olds engaged and not crying while also holding the attention of the fifth and sixth graders.

For Jeannie's continuing education that year, she went to the children's ministry conference at Saddleback Church in California. Even though that congregation is very different from ours, Jeannie got ideas that have shaped our ministry to this day. One of the speakers there captured her imagination.

"Whether it is right or wrong," he said, "parents today value having to pay for their kid's activities. If they pay to play soccer, T-ball, or dance, they will make sure their children attend. They also equate paying with value and commitment."

Pay for activities? Our folks at FBC had never been asked to pay for anything. If taking on tradition wasn't risky enough, charging for activities would certainly turn up the heat. And yet, what the folks at Saddleback were saying seemed to ring true to Jeannie.

She began to pray about where to go with our children's summer ministries. She decided to make the shift to a "camp" format. Every kid likes to go to camp. What better place for camp than at "my church"? At a meeting open to all parents, Jeannie laid out her vision for what would become Camp Creation and Camp Jonah. While not clear yet on every detail, she cashed in every chip she had and asked the parents to trust her in this new journey, promising a path of deeper spiritual growth for their kids.

Her passion and transparency paid off. The fifty to sixty parents who attended the meeting were excited by the vision that was painted for them and wanted to be a part of making it happen. They became ambassadors for the vision within the church. Even the traditionalists were on board when they recognized the authentic desire to create an environment that would be most effective in helping our children to grow deeper in their faith and also to reach out more intentionally beyond our church and into our community.

Today, Camp Creation for preschoolers runs from Tuesday through Thursday from 9 a.m. to 11:30 a.m. This is "just right" for the little ones as the lessons, songs, games, and crafts are all planned for preschoolers. The message is consistent from year to year: 1) God made the world, 2) God made me and loves me, and 3) God wants me to love others. The counselors for this camp include moms and dads, a few older members of the congregation, and some of the youth from our church. We charge less than $20 for Camp Creation for which the children receive a T-shirt, snacks, some keepsake crafts, and a goodie bag of lesson reinforcements at the end of camp.

Camp Jonah is for first through sixth grades. We like to think of it as Extreme VBS! Camp runs for five days from 9 a.m. to 2 p.m. The day opens with high-energy worship, and then classes move through a set of electives that include sports, Bible study, game time, Bible drills, and others. The day ends with worship and wrap-up of lessons learned. Many of our older youth serve as counselors along with parents and other adults. Each youth counselor or adult works with a group of six to eight kids through the week, building friendships with and among the kids, talking about Jesus and making connections between what they learn at Camp Jonah and how to apply it to their lives. These small groups are the life blood of Camp Jonah. The fee for this camp is $60 for the week and includes lunch each day, a T-shirt, keepsake crafts, and a Big Friday Celebration.

Charging fees for these camps was not met with great enthusiasm, but the fees allowed us to offer a much higher quality experience for the kids. Anonymous scholarships are always available for children who need them.

So, how does one measure the worth of such a huge shift? Jeannie offers three metrics. First, the kids love it. They invite their friends and look forward to Camp Jonah the minute school is out.

Second, the parents love it because the children love it—and their kids get it! Whatever the message is, the children absorb it because it is shared with them in many different ways throughout each day of camp.

One little girl came home from Camp Jonah one day. Her grandmother was about to sweep the kitchen, but the little girl stopped her. "Let me do that, Grammy," she said. "We learned at Camp Jonah that God wants me to be a helper when I can."

That story has been repeated many times in many different homes. Those action-oriented nuggets of truth are tag lines each day in the Camp Jonah experience—short and memorable, repeated and reinforced.

A third measure of success is the number of children participating. It has simply exploded. In less than ten years we have gone from seventy kids in VBS to more than 420 children in the two camps, 176 in Camp Creation and 245 in Camp Jonah. A large number of those children are not part of our congregation, and many have no church affiliation. All of these children are learning of God's love for them and God's calling on them to live as his disciples.

With some success under her belt, the next thing Jeannie tackled was our Wednesday evening children's program. For years we had the traditional Baptist missions training of RAs (Royal Ambassadors), GAs (Girls in Action), and Mission Friends. We also had a graded choir program. We struggled to keep our numbers in the mid-thirties for birth to sixth grade. Leaders did not like the curriculum. There was no energy. Like everyone else, we were also competing with sports, dance, and homework for the time and attention of our children and families.

But because we valued this time for discipleship, Jeannie knew that she had to make FBC "the place to be on Wednesday nights." After much prayer, she decided that if the model for the camps was so inviting, why not do something similar on Wednesdays? Now called Cross Training Kids, discipleship on Wednesday nights begins with music and singing followed by a video introduction to the night's lesson. The preschoolers follow a similar track in another part of the building.

Missions are a major focus on Wednesday nights, with three mission projects undertaken each semester: one for our church, one for the community, and a third one for the world. The kids really take ownership of these mission efforts. We have seen their sacrifice and a giving that comes straight from the heart.

One day Jeannie received an email from one of the elementary-age girls. She told Jeannie about a rundown area of town that she would ride past in the car each week and how it made her so sad. "But then I thought, 'Hey, I can make a difference. I learned that in Cross Training!'" She asked her teacher at school if she could set an envelope out on her desk and collect money for people who are poor. The wise and compassionate teacher said, "Yes."

"I collected $10.62," the young girl wrote proudly. I'm just emailing you to see if you have any idea what I can do with the money so that it can help a lot of people."

Hands-on mission learning—my church, my community, my world . . .

Like Camp Jonah, small groups are the key to Cross Training Kids. In most cases, an adult stays with the same group of girls or boys from first through sixth grades, building lasting relationships with the kids over a long period of time. The small group is a time and place where kids get to talk about what is happening in their world and relate it to all they are learning about God and faith.

In a recent semester, 120 elementary-aged kids and more than forty preschoolers participated in Cross Training. The energy on Wednesday nights rocks the house!

When asked what lessons she has learned over the last thirteen years, Jeannie offered these:

• Above all else, teach the heart and not the head.
• It is okay to have fun at church. It doesn't mean you have to water down God's story or his message.
• Get all the ideas you can from other churches. We're all on the same team.
• Ask kids for their ideas. They are smart.
• Use technology. Find someone who knows how to do it well and learn from that person.
• Kids and adults crave meaningful relationships. Give them that chance.
• Thank your volunteers. Respect their time and pray for them.
• Don't be afraid to change. Keep looking around the corner for whatever is next.

Adult Spiritual Formation

Jayne Davis is one of the brightest people with whom I have ever worked. She had to be. When she came to work at FBC on a part-time basis as minister for spiritual formation, she was the mother of four children and a full-time student at Campbell Divinity School. While her husband, Wes, was a great help, she clearly had way too much on her plate. Yet she was tireless in her efforts to lead our adult Sunday school to be an effective tool for discipleship. She studied and read about other churches and new models they had introduced for this purpose. She visited some of those churches and had long in-depth conversations with their leaders. Then with great care and deliberation she would implement new ideas at

FBC. While each of them had a measure of success, none of them were what she wanted for FBC.

To say that she was discouraged fails to capture her angst. She even came to the place where she thought about resigning, quitting her work at FBC. With every new idea she launched, the rest of our staff and I supported her. Even when I thought something might not work, I encouraged her to move forward. If we were going to be true to the idea that we can try anything, then we had to let Jayne try anything.

In the midst of one of our five-year strategic planning processes, the team of clergy and laity took seriously the charge to discern where God was leading our church and came to the conclusion that we needed to focus our attention on discipleship. In short, we needed to spend more time with Jesus. If we were going to be missional, we needed to spend time with the one who embodies missional.

To this end, we decided to spend six months with Jesus, immersing ourselves as a congregation in the four Gospels. We believed that if we followed Jesus along the way in his life and ministry in Scripture, we would understand how to follow him more intentionally in our own lives and in our life together. We had an idea of what this might look like from a preaching standpoint, but we were not certain what to do with Sunday school.

Someone on the team spoke up. That person recalled how some years earlier when we had done *40 Days of Purpose*, one of the best things about that experience was that the sermons and Sunday school lessons focused on the same text. In worship you got to hear the word being proclaimed. In Sunday school you tried to figure out what to do with it in your own life. Another person recalled how the daily readings during *40 Days* had everyone "on the same page" and what great energy and conversation that created week to week. All of that was easy to do, of course, when someone else was producing all the material. But neither Jayne nor any of the other staff members knew of a readily available resource that could take us through the four Gospels in six months in any format, let alone one like *40 Days of Purpose*.

It was then that a fateful question was asked: "Why can't we write our own material?" Just beginning to imagine what such an effort might require, some folks sought to slow down that train. One person argued that it would be boring to hear the same thing in Sunday school and then to plow that ground again in worship. Another wondered where we would find all of these writers. But this was an idea that had already left the station.

"We can do anything for six months," we decided. "Who knows? Maybe it will even be cheaper to produce our own stuff rather than buying it."

And so it was agreed. We would embark on a six-month journey with Jesus. We called it "Along the Way," because that seemed to capture the life and ministry of Jesus. Jesus did not appear to get up each morning with an extensive and detailed "to do" list. Rather, the whole of Jesus' life was focused on being at God's disposal, ready to make God known, often in the very ordinary situations of daily life, by what he said, what he did, and how he cared for people. And that is the example we wanted to follow.

We found some wonderfully gifted writers who had been in our midst all along. They crafted some of the finest Sunday school lessons I have ever read. When it came to the daily devotions, Jayne had to ask a much wider spectrum of people to participate. She needed nearly thirty folks a month to do that. With energy and enthusiasm, people began to write about faith—their faith—longtime members, new members, young, old, men, women, those who were celebrating, those who were struggling, those who were seeking. More new writers were discovered in the process. To be sure, there was some editing to be done by Jayne, and there were a couple of folks with confused theology. But in the end, the product produced each month was of high quality by any measure.

Even though the preachers and the Sunday school writers used the same text for each Sunday, the sermons and the lessons seemed to complement each other rather than repeating the same material. The early service crowd rolled into Sunday school having already worshipped. The later service group always wanted to know what the preacher had said about this or that. It enriched the discussion and learning in that hour. Once again, everyone was on the same page.

One of our deacons told of being at a Rotary Club meeting one day. He sat at a table for eight, three of whom were members at FBC. One of them asked of the other two what they thought about the *Along the Way* devotion for that particular morning. After the exchange of ideas, another person at the table asked what they were talking about. It gave the three of them a chance to talk about their church, their faith, and "trying to follow Jesus" with people with whom they might never have had such a conversation.

Halfway through that six-month journey, a decision needed to be made. Was this a temporary experiment, or had a new way of doing Sunday school emerged at FBC? I'll never forget Jayne saying to the staff, "I don't think we will ever go back to buying Sunday school literature again."

Today, more than five years later, the members of FBC still write their own Sunday school material, every week, week after week. There are several reasons for that.

Writing our own material helps us to guide the discipleship conversation. It's hard to lead change or cast vision for discipleship when every Sunday school class is focused on something different.

Most importantly, though, writing this material has shaped us. When folks are asked to write a devotional, it affirms in them that God speaks through them, that God has a word to say to the body through them, that they have a role to play in encouraging the congregation in their faith. Many would not necessarily have thought that of themselves without this experience. That does something to a person.

When others in the congregation read the devotions that have been written, it is powerful and humbling to realize that such faith surrounds us in our church family. These aren't the typical conversations we have with one another standing in the hallway or waiting for the worship service to start.

Along the Way is revealing our faith to us and is helping us to cultivate a culture of mutual discipleship where we walk alongside each other in our faith journey. It makes room for the voices of children and adults, teenagers and prisoners, recovering alcoholics, those who are grieving or in pain, those who are at the top of their game, and those who have recently been homeless—all of us, together.

A young man, named Cory, was an inmate in our county jail. He was greatly encouraged in his faith by one of our men who visits the jail. Cory loved *Along the Way* so, when he was transferred to a prison out of state, we made sure to mail the material to him each month. One day Jayne emailed Cory and asked him if he would write one of our devotions. Scripture passages are randomly assigned to individuals who agree to write devotions, and Cory's was no different. The passage he received was from the book of Genesis and the story of Joseph, specifically the reunion of Joseph with his brothers after spending so many years in prison. Cory wrote about forgiveness and what it does to you when you harbor a lack of forgiveness in your heart. From a jail cell, Cory discipled us on forgiveness. Around here, we call that a "God thing."

Writing your own curriculum materials is not an easy undertaking. The production cost of producing hundreds of booklets, it turns out, is "not" a money saver for the church. The dollar cost is about the same, and the recruitment of writers and the editing and production take a good bit of time. We have to work further ahead in the calendar than any of us realized, which requires a great deal of planning and organization. It is a major commitment of time and energy, and a challenge to maintain a fresh word to say.

When we began, I was fairly certain that we could not sustain this kind of effort for more than eighteen months or so. But Jayne had finally come upon a tool, a way of doing discipleship that captured the imagination and the hearts of our church members. They love being on the same page. They love receiving the insights and encouragement that come from their fellow members.

We didn't intentionally set out to take on the sacred cow of traditional Sunday School curriculum, but the openness of our people to give up what they are used to in order to allow God to do something more in their midst has changed us and shaped us in ways that we are still coming to understand.

It takes courage to lead change, and it is seldom easy. Both Jayne and Jeannie had the requisite courage to lead in their individual ministries. People have to trust those who lead change. Jeannie and Jayne earned that trust. When it came time to jettison long-standing programs for children and for our Sunday school, it was that same trust that allowed us to try new ways of doing and being. It really was a new way of doing church.

Cultivating Hopeful Imagination

Pay attention to the Spirit. As you read this story, what did the Spirit prompt in you regarding your own congregation and context?

• Whispers: How is God stirring up your imagination?
• Groans: What needs in your church or community do you think about?
• Praises: What resources or individuals or opportunities come to mind?

Identify sacred cows. Not all traditions are sacred cows that need to be put out to pasture. Many traditions have endured for a long time for good reason: they are meaningful and fruitful.

Sacred cows are those programs and practices that are revered for their own sake, not necessarily for the kingdom value they actually hold. They are the programs that are immune from question or criticism. And while they may have started off with a good and noble purpose or were highly relevant at a particular period of time, their season has passed. Sometimes we can't even recall how they got started; they've just always been.

These sacred cows can become barriers to the new things God wants to do in us and among us in our congregation—ends in and of themselves instead of means to a greater end.

- What are the sacred cows in the life of your congregation?
- What might new growth in that ministry area look like if "the way we've always done it" made room for new ways of doing church?

Acknowledge the culture clash. We can lament all of the activities that consume the schedules of our children and families, but to what end? Our culture has shifted, and bemoaning that fact does little to change it. Instead, we can find creative ways to help our people who are "on the go" —for work, for travel soccer, for dance competitions—to be grounded in their faith; to see wherever they are as their mission field, and to equip them to be influencers for Christ in those places.

Our transitions in children's ministry affirmed for us that, for all of the pulls on their time and attention, kids are still hungry for spiritual truth and godly relationships. We need to be more intentional about speaking their language in ways they can hear.

- Where are you frustrated or competing with culture?
- How can you adapt some of your discipleship efforts to meet the needs and realities of a mobile society?
- How can you refresh and retool some of your programs to speak more effectively to a new generation?

Be patient in sowing seeds. Most of us are happy to sow seeds. It is a hallmark of ministry and a hopeful process. Our unspoken expectation in this endeavor, though, is that the seeds we sow will be the fast-growing kind, bearing fruit in the same season if possible.

At FBC, several years of ministry without much in the way of seedlings emerging from the soil were hard. Maybe you've been there; maybe you're there now—where you're wondering if anything you're doing is making any difference. Don't give up too soon.

Remember first that growth is not our task. That is God's department. Our job is to faithfully keep sowing the seeds. Moses sowed seeds among the Israelites for forty years wandering in the desert and never got to see the promised land. It's an unpopular God truth, but it puts our work in perspective. We need to find our purpose in the journey.

In the midst of that, though, remember also the Chinese bamboo tree. No matter how meticulously you tend to its care, any growth in the plant is imperceptible. In the first year, or the second year, even in the third and fourth years of watering and fertilizing and tending, it appears as if nothing is happening. But in year five, the Chinese bamboo tree grows with abandon—an amazing eighty feet tall! While nothing appeared to be happening on the surface, an extensive root system was developing underground to support the growth that was getting ready to happen.

• Where are you discouraged, sowing seeds that do not appear to be taking root?
• What is God's purpose in the sowing that you do, irrespective of the outcome of that work?
• Who might help you to look at your ministry "field" with fresh eyes?
• Who is someone with eyes to see the emerging seedlings that perhaps you have been overlooking?

Allow for the freedom to fail. Creativity and innovation in ministry entail risk. Not everything will work or turn out exactly as you hoped it would—the first time, the second time, or even the third or fourth time. Great inventors readily dismiss the notion of failure. They prefer to say that they successfully discovered a lot of things that didn't work before stumbling upon the thing that did. There must be a freedom to fail if any worthwhile risks are going to be undertaken in ministry.

- How do you foster an environment that encourages innovative ministry?
- How tolerant are you of unsuccessful ideas?
- Do you truly grant a freedom to fail?

Ask and encourage challenging faith questions. It is our challenge as staff to create an environment in preaching and in teaching where questions are embraced and where it is safe for folks to examine and wonder about the things they believe. One of the benefits of writing our own adult Sunday school curriculum has been the opportunity to give direction to that discipleship conversation.

Most of the people in our congregation—and in yours—know and believe the story of Jesus Christ. It is deeply important to them. But many are unsure how to be set free by it. While stories inspire us with what is possible, questions challenge the boundaries that we put up around what we will allow faith to be in our lives.

Jesus asked great questions. They are powerful questions because—in typical Jesus fashion—it is our own answers to those questions that will change us: "What do you want me to do for you?" "Who do you say that I am?" "What are you looking for?"

These questions are unsettling. They are messy. They presuppose that faith makes an important difference in what happens next in our day-to-day living and in our churches. Sometimes I believe we have stopped imagining that it does.

- Are we asking questions that invite people to live in expectation of Jesus showing up in our midst?

Changing How We See Ourselves

The church exists primarily for those who are not a part of it.

There are things we believe about ourselves as a church that can limit what God is able to do through us and in us. But that doesn't have to be the end of the story. A few key decisions can change the trajectory of your congregation; how it sees itself and understands its role in the community.

The front page of the morning newspaper told the story in the bleakest of terms. Good Shepherd Center, a ministry devoted to helping the hungry and homeless in our community, was now homeless itself. The ministry had been started by a handful of individuals concerned about hungry folks they encountered on the streets of Wilmington, and was housed in a small Episcopal church a few blocks from First Baptist. A lot of other churches, including ours, supported the ministry with finances and volunteers. It was essentially a soup kitchen serving lunch and a day shelter where folks could bathe, get their mail, find a little work, and generally survive.

Members of the church where the ministry was housed felt that they needed to reclaim the space for their own needs. A local AME Zion church had offered to house the ministry. But when the word got out, folks in that particular neighborhood protested and the offer was rescinded. The future of Good Shepherd was very much up in the air.

After reading the article about its dilemma, Jim Everette and I wondered if our downtown kitchen might suffice for Good Shepherd's needs until it found a new home. We kicked the idea around for a few minutes, thinking about all the hurdles we would have to clear for such a thing to work. Jim said he would call the leaders and see if they might have an interest.

Three minutes later, Jim was back in my office. "They are on their way," Jim said. "Something has happened. Kathy was in tears, really crying. They will be here in five minutes." Kathy was Kathy Dawson, executive director of Good Shepherd. With her when she arrived were the chair of the board and another volunteer. Kathy's eyes were still red from crying. Jim and I were a bit puzzled.

Kathy Dawson and Don Hassenflo unpacked for us an emotional explanation of the morning's events. They had been in an emergency board meeting called to discuss their plight. Amid half-eaten pastries and empty coffee cups, they found themselves reduced to prayer. They had approached several smaller churches about hosting Good Shepherd. They had looked at warehouse space. It seemed as though no one wanted the center's clientele in their neighborhood. So they prayed. The prayer was simple: "Lord, we are at the end of our rope. We do not know what to do next. If you want us to continue this ministry, you will have to provide us a place."

With those words the meeting ended, and a discouraged and defeated board of directors began to move on toward their own places of work. Kathy was weeping. She felt like a failure. Others were seeking to console her by assuring her that it was not her fault. As she made her way to her office, deprived of any shred of hope, her assistant told her that Jim Everette was on the phone holding for her. When Kathy answered the phone, Jim asked if they had a place to relocate and, if they didn't, did she think the kitchen and Fireside Hall at FBC might work for them.

Don said, "We are just not accustomed to getting our prayers answered this quickly."

I told him that this was just exploratory on our part, but we were serious about taking the idea to our church leadership if the three of them thought the space would work. But I still had one question I wanted answered before we toured the space.

"You said that you had explored every option you could imagine and that you had spoken with more than a dozen churches. You never called us. Why not?"

After some nervous glances at one another, Kathy said: "We never dreamed you would be open to this. We did not think any of the 'big steeple churches' would do this kind of ministry. You know it can be a rough crowd some days, and not always the cleanest."

Well, of course, we knew her crowd. Jim and I, along with several of our members, had volunteered at Good Shepherd. But we knew what she meant. Jim and I were not certain that our leaders would go for the idea, but we were hopeful they would and we were willing to ask.

We showed Kathy and Don the tiny kitchen and realized it was a good bit larger than the one they were using currently. The dining room was three times the size of theirs. They were ecstatic at the possibilities. We told them we could only do the soup kitchen part of the ministry and that we would need church approval for that. (We have a congregational polity in the Baptist church, and in big decisions everyone has a vote.) We promised to get back to them promptly.

At our next diaconate meeting we rolled out our proposal, complete with all the reservations and potential problems we saw. We told of our plan to send a letter to all of our downtown neighbors stating our intent to house the soup kitchen for an indeterminate amount of time. We would point out that every day (Monday through Friday), a crowd of more than 200 would line up on Fifth Avenue to wait for lunch to be served in the church.

Jim and I made the best case we could to the deacons. There were only a handful of questions asked and answered. Then it was time for a vote.

"Any more questions?" the chair of deacons asked. The silence in the room was finally broken by one of our deacons, a district court judge.

"If we can't say 'yes' to this request, we may as well shut the doors because we would not be much of a church." The vote was unanimous in the affirmative.

Katrina Knight, the current executive director of Good Shepherd Center, recently told a group her take on that story. "First Baptist started from 'yes,'" she said. "Our soup kitchen was homeless, and we were in danger of not having this program. They came to the table with us and figured out how to make this work."

Reflecting on that decision of the diaconate some years later, Vick Griffin, the chair at the time of the vote, said: "Something was different that night; something had changed. The discussion centered not on why we shouldn't do something like this but, instead, what do we have to do to make this happen. So, we jumped in with both feet and for the next year and a half, five days a week, we had church members down at the church giving of their time."

Indeed, something had changed. In some ways the whole thing wasn't that big of a deal, but in other ways it was a huge shift in focus for FBC. As Vick told the deacons the night of the vote, "We have just made a big decision for our church, but I am convinced that we would not have made this decision five years ago. We have come a long way."

He was right. It was as though our congregation had spent years getting ready for a moment just like this.

Jim Everette reminded everyone that voting "yes" was the easy part, but that actually hosting Good Shepherd was going to require a whole lot more of all of us. Jim had worked hard in the past at getting volunteers for Good Shepherd, but he had had limited success. The facility was not in the best part of town, and many of our folks were simply afraid to go there. When Jim would ask FBC folks, "How about serving at the soup kitchen?" more often than not he received responses such as "It's dangerous there" or "That's a scary place."

But now the soup kitchen was coming to our place. No excuses!

Good Shepherd already had a fine cadre of volunteers, including some of our folks. But our setting was different from where they had previously worked and served. Anyone who entered our building had access to the whole place, so security became an immediate issue. Someone suggested uniformed officers, but that did not feel terribly hospitable. Jim determined to solve the matter with volunteers from the church. Folks sat at small tables in the two halls where guests might wander into other parts of the building. When they did, our hosts asked how they could help them find what they were looking for. More often than not, they were simply looking for a rest room.

Although we had no showers in our rest rooms, having a toilet and a clean place to shave, brush teeth, and take sponge baths meant the world to our guests. Yes, the rest rooms were overworked, but you just cannot invite folks into your house and then not treat them like guests.

Good Shepherd already had cooking teams in place. Our folks would serve as hosts. They welcomed our guests at the main entrance every day. They put out "butt cans" at the door since we are a smoke-free facility. The teams prepared the food, and we served the meal and cleaned up each day. Our folks were simply terrific.

But perhaps the best idea Jim had was to recruit people to just sit at the tables and eat with and talk to our guests. One of our most determined "missionaries" was a young woman named Christina. She was like any other woman in her early twenties except that Christina was quadriplegic. She was the victim of an automobile accident shortly after her sixteenth birthday and was left with no movement below her neck. Confined to a bed or wheelchair for the rest of her life, Christina had the mind of Christ and a desire to serve as his presence however she could.

Greeting hungry guests in need of a kind word and a smile as much as a meal, Christina and her parents put forth an incredible effort to serve as greeters on a regular basis.

Every Friday, seated in her wheelchair, with her ventilator on, Christina would smile as folks came through the door and say "Welcome."

As the weeks went by, our guests looked forward to seeing Christina sitting at the door, ready to brighten their day. Folks coming for lunch began to hug her as they came into the building.

"You can't fight them off," Jim joked with her one day.

"I don't want to," she said.

I'm not sure that I was ever prouder of First Baptist than I was when we hosted the soup kitchen. Day after day, week after week, and month after month our folks came. More than 100 of our members became involved in this very "hands on" ministry.

For more than eighteen months we served lunch at the corner of Fifth and Market to whomever showed up. Was there some risk in opening our church up like that? Certainly. Our deacons could have balked. The congregation could have said "no." The neighbors could have resisted. None of that happened. We believe that God gave us an opportunity and we said "yes," not knowing exactly how it would turn out. Quite simply, it could not have gone better.

During that time, the board at Good Shepherd developed plans for a new home for the ministry. Today, the center has a fine facility that includes not only the soup kitchen but also a night shelter for men and women, transitional housing, and even a small medical clinic.

When the time came to move into the center's new building, though the location was still not in the best part of town, many of our folks said, "They are not going without me!" Good Shepherd and its guests had become a part of us. Our volunteers went with the ministry to its new location, and many of them continue to serve there today.

We have other FBC folks who drive a truck to area restaurants to pick up donated food in the "Second Helpings Ministry" for Good Shepherd and several who help with dinner at the overnight shelter.

None of this is "owned" or controlled by FBC, but I suspect we shall always feel as though it is simply an extension of our church family. To our way of thinking, it is the best of what missional partnerships look like in our community.

When you begin to relate to people who are different from you, who live in different neighborhoods than you, who come from different backgrounds than you, you quickly learn that they are not that different after all. Barriers get broken down. Understanding deepens. Friendships bloom in unlikely soil.

Opening the doors of our church to the soup kitchen changed how the community saw FBC. It also changed us. If we could do that, we felt like we could do most anything. A lot of churches in every city open their doors like this, but a lot don't. What an opportunity is missed when that simple act of hospitality is not offered. And in the end, it really is just hospitality.

Caring for the City

One day the district attorney in our county called with a strange, but compelling, request. Ben David was concerned about the families of homicide victims. The courthouse was right around the corner from our church, but it was a painful place for people who came to attend the trials of those accused of killing their loved ones. Ben, a Presbyterian layman, wondered if we could make space available at the church for those families to meet each month with personnel from his office. We did. Now, once a year those same families gather in our church for a memorial service of remembrance.

All of this morphed into a new identity for FBC in downtown Wilmington.

When we did the Hopeful Imagination conference, one of the participants was the long-time mayor of Wilmington, Billy Saffo, a member of the Greek Orthodox Church. He came to speak to the many community partnerships of which FBC had been a part through the years. He said the city looked upon FBC as a "partner" in caring for the city. We could not help but think back to what Dr. Doug Bailey had told us. For all the criticism the church had faced across the years, here was the mayor thanking us for being partners in solving problems and meeting needs. He said, "When we have a unique problem for which we in city government are ill-equipped to handle, one of the first places we call is First Baptist Church." Hospitality.

We were intentional in cultivating those relationships with community leaders. When something important needs to happen in the community, even and especially if a crisis occurs, it makes all the difference in the world that those relationships are already in place, that familiarity and trust already exist, so that meaningful conversations can take place that lead to action.

One of the ways we do this is with our annual Mayor's Prayer Breakfast. Each year on a weekday morning near President's Day in February, we invite every elected official in the county and its municipalities to breakfast. Some men in our church cook pancakes, bacon, and sausage.

A different elected official is invited each year to talk about how his or her faith impacts his or her service to the community. We've had speakers who serve in the state legislature, our congressman, the mayor, judges, county commissioners, and others. We even had the governor of North Carolina one year. The event is never political. We never invite someone to speak who is campaigning for office that year. It is about the role of faith in the lives of people in the public arena. And in the end, it is about specifically praying for these people who are willing to serve.

I'll never forget running into a district court judge in a sandwich shop one day at lunch. She made her way over to where I was seated and said, "I just want to thank you and First Baptist for hosting the prayer breakfast each year. So far as I know, it is the only time and place where anyone ever prays for me and the very difficult and serious work I do." She went on to say, "That is why I never miss one."

Across the years, Jim Everette made a habit of asking the question wherever he went in the city: "What do you need and how can we help?" We were willing to partner with anyone to those common ends.

An office of the drug court is located next door to our church in the Harrelson Center. People who are passing through that office are tested and counseled in the hope that they avoid ever being back in court again. Classes for the group are held in our church. People who have lost a family member to suicide meet in a support group. People who suffer from obsessive compulsive disorder meet regularly at our church. Classes for soon-to-be teenage parents are taught by WIRE at FBC so that they might be better prepared to care for the children who will change their lives. For FBC, all of these ministries fall under the umbrella of hospitality. The strangers who come our way are made to feel welcomed and at home in our midst. We do our best to avoid being judgmental. This seems like the work of Jesus.

For years our church has been a strong and stable partner with Cape Fear Habitat for Humanity. We sponsor and build a house every other year in partnership with Pine Valley United Methodist Church. While Habitat for Humanity is clearly a Christian ministry, recently FBC was asked to partner in a multi-faith build. People from the Buddhist temple, Jewish synagogue, Islamic mosque, and Christian churches worked together on a build. Partnering with hospitality has become a hallmark of FBC.

One of the most wonderful ministries launched by Jim Everette and FBC is our twice-a-year Mission Possible Days. Akin to what my friend David Crocker has done with his Operation Inasmuch Ministry, Mission Possible was our effort to fan out into the city wherever there was a need. From pouring a concrete basketball court at the shelter house for abused and neglected children to cleaning and painting the local food bank warehouse, from putting new roofs on leaking houses to cleaning up an elderly member's yard, from sorting clothes delivered to a clothing closet to repair work at a local school, FBC members engage the community.

One day a retired Methodist minister who often worshipped with us stopped by our church office to invite us to join other churches in starting the Wilmington Interfaith Hospitality Network (WIHN). We were asked to be one of thirteen churches to provide shelter for homeless families for one week at a time four times a year. We would never have more than four families or fourteen people at a time. We would provide a private place for each family to sleep, shower and bathroom facilities, and an evening meal. Two church members (male and female) were required to spend the night when we were the host church.

When Jim first floated the idea with our mission and ministry committee, he was met with a good bit of resistance. One committee member, Wanda, wondered aloud: "If we take these kinds of people into our church, they might burn the building down or steal something—and we just couldn't allow that."

Jim offered a lower threshold of ministry. "How about if we become a support church?" We would provide meals and people to sleep over if another church needed help in that area.

Wanda, one of the most "missional" people I have ever known, volunteered to serve in one of the other churches. At a subsequent committee meeting, she said "You know what? Those are just the sweetest people. I hate that we missed the opportunity to host them at FBC."

Shortly after that, one of the original churches had to withdraw from the ministry. Wanda was the one who led the charge for our church to take its place. She said of her experience as a support church volunteer:

"I just fell in love with those people. I found out they were just like I was. They were just people who were struggling to keep their family, their children, and their lives together. God has changed my heart about this ministry and given me the desire to work with these families. I get much more out of it than they do."

One of our couples working in this ministry, a retired school superintendent and his retired teacher wife, told Jim they were going to be out of town the next time we were scheduled to host WIHN. They asked if he could swap weeks with another church so they could be there. He told them not to worry. He was sure he could find someone to take their place. They protested that he didn't understand their request. They did not want a replacement. They didn't want to miss their turn with the families.

A young businessman who volunteers with WIHN was helping unload the roll-away beds from the trailer as the Sunday afternoon transition from the last week's host church to us took place. He said of our guests, "They make a home wherever they are. I come home sometimes and ask myself, 'Am I truly making a home within my house?'" Perhaps this is a question we should all ask of ourselves. As with so many ministries, we really do get more out of it than we give.

As Wanda told the folks in her deacon workshop at the Hopeful Imagination conference: "When God reaches in and changes your heart, things will start happening at your church."

Caring for One Another

When you are the preacher and you stand in front of people week after week, you notice things—odd things. A wonderful young couple in our church, Stuart and Becky, seemed to never show up on the same Sunday. He would be in worship one week and she the next. After this went on for several weeks, it seemed obvious that something was amiss in their relationship. So I called Stuart, told him what I had noticed and asked if anything was wrong.

He excused himself to close his office door, and then he said, "Mike, its Abbey." Abbey was their precious and beautiful three-year-old daughter. He went on to explain the heartbreaking experience he and his wife had lived through since they brought her home from the hospital as a newborn. "One of us has to be with her at all times. So one of us goes to Sunday school and stays with her through the extended session, and the other goes to worship. The next week we trade off. Mike, she never sleeps more than forty minutes at a time. One of us has to sleep with her every night. We have known something was wrong, but we finally got the diagnosis last week: she has Rett syndrome."

As he went on to explain the details of this wretched condition that attacks only girls, I began to imagine what the three years had been like for this family. It became a tearful conversation for both of us. I told Stuart that I was coming to their house that evening to meet with them. He protested that it was not necessary. I told him that it might not be necessary for them, but it was for me.

In their home that evening I saw what the Rett's had done to Abbey. While I will not share those details, what I saw left me brokenhearted. I made a promise to them that night to do something. Abbey was getting the care she needed, but I was concerned for her parents. How were they coping? Who was looking out for these two exhausted souls?

As the staff began to talk about our options, one of the things we did was to look around the church. We became aware of several families who have "special needs" children, including those with Down syndrome and Prader-Willi syndrome. One family has a son who is confined to a wheelchair. He's blind, has never walked or spoken, and is tube-fed.

We decided to form a support group for these parents. We asked Fred and Janet Nelson, the parents of another Abbey, to give leadership. Their Abbey was born deaf. With the help of cochlear implants and cued speech, Abbey learned to communicate. But the Nelsons knew what it was like dealing with doctors and things with their children that could not be fixed. The coming together of that group proved to be a blessing to each family.

About the same time all of this was happening, we had read about an initiative by the McLean Bible Church in McLean, Virginia. Its leaders had started a certification process for churches desiring to become an "access church." This meant that we would do everything possible to make sure we not only had physical access for all persons at our church, but also that everyone would be cared for spiritually—that they would have the same access as everyone else.

A new Sunday school class was formed for the children with special needs. They had a really cool room that was easy to access. Their class was called the God Squad, and they were one proud group. Everything was designed to affirm God's love for them and our love for them and their families.

Back in those days, each year we had a different theme for the year. Clearly the most memorable theme was the "Year of Special Needs." One of the things we realized from the parents of the kids was that people had a hard time understanding their situations. People did not know what to say or how to relate to them. So, once a month, as a part of our worship, we introduced each of these children and their parents to the congregation. Then in an effort not to be exploitative or to cause embarrassment, someone would escort the children from the room. Then I would interview the parents about their child. The results were amazing.

When Abbey's parents told her story, every person in worship that day was touched. Toward the end of the interview I asked her daddy if there was anything we as a church could do for Abbey or for them. I'll never forget Stuart's words: "I just hope some of you will invite our daughter to your child's birthday party."

One of the great moments in my life came when Abbey's daddy and I baptized her. If we were going to be an "access church," she was going to have access to the baptistery, too.

When the parents of Kyle, the boy in the wheelchair, came to be interviewed, they shared the details of the brain damage that occurred during his birth that left him profoundly disabled. When I asked what we as a church could do, his father, Donald, said that people in the church had been great to them since they had moved to Wilmington. Many had helped with Kyle's care. But he did have one request: "When you see us coming with Kyle in his wheelchair, please don't walk the other way or look away from us. Feel free to speak to him and to us."

The very next week I encountered the family hustling their way to Sunday school. "Running late?" I asked. "Yes," they replied. "We have created a monster. Every family we have seen from the parking lot to the sidewalk to the hallway has stopped to talk to Kyle." Donald then looked at me and asked, "Do you know how cool that is?"

It was in telling those stories that we changed as a church. Their stories became our stories. We were an access church. We really did care about not only the special needs children, but also their parents. We began to see ourselves differently. The things we did in the name of Jesus really did make a difference in the world.

Doing Whatever It Takes

In 1996 the Wilmington area endured two direct hits from sister hurricanes Bertha and Fran. Both Category 3 storms took their toll. Bertha brought massive rains and saturated the ground with moisture. With the ground softened up from those rains, Fran's brutal winds took down huge trees and power lines in every part of the city. Both times the North Carolina Baptist Men (and Women) showed up the very next day. They prepared and served food to anyone who needed a hot meal. These servants of God came from Baptist churches all over the state. They were truly God's angels to our community. We did our best to make them feel at home.

During Bertha, they set up their mobile kitchen and portable showers at our activities center. Electrical repairmen came from all over the southeast working to restore power as quickly as possible. They worked long and grueling shifts; and when it came time for a break, they needed a place to sleep. We used our gym to set up a makeshift motel. The local power company brought in dozens of roll-away beds. The women of our church took to the mall and wherever to find bed linens.

Since these burly linemen were working twelve-hour-plus shifts, after they ate and showered, they settled in for few hours rest on their Mickey Mouse- and Cinderella-themed bed covers. And there was always a chocolate candy on every pillow.

We had folks cycling through the gym all day and all night, both to sleep and to change out the linens. Our members who had electric power would wash the sheets and towels and bring them back for the next crew. It was an amazing thing to watch—and to hear. Forty grown men snoring at the same time makes for quite the sound.

When the Baptist Men prepared meals, they served them on site to those in need. The Red Cross partnered with them to deliver meals into places where people had no power with which to cook. My son told of riding on one of the Red Cross trucks and passing out meals through a side window one night down at Carolina Beach. The only light was that coming from the Red Cross vehicle. People would emerge out of the shadows to receive the meals needed for their families. Always they said, "Thank you . . . and God bless you." This work went on for days in the aftermath of both storms.

But it was Hurricane Fran that will be forever remembered in the history of First Baptist. Her potent winds on a dark Thursday night took down the 125-year-old primary steeple of our downtown church. A dozen or more members showed up the next morning to help with the debris cleanup. Needless to say, we were all a bit preoccupied with our downed steeple, not to mention the downed trees and damages at our own homes. With the downtown sanctuary temporarily condemned, we worshipped at our activities center the next Sunday.

Given our situation, the North Carolina Baptist Men had set up this time at our sister church, Winter Park Baptist. By Monday afternoon, I had attended to everything I needed to do and thought it might be a good idea to go over to Winter Park to say "thank you" to those who had come to our aid. A light drizzle had begun as darkness set in. What I found at Winter Park that evening blessed my soul. Most of the workers had settled in for the evening, but out in the dimness of their parking lot I saw five of our members. Two of them were unable to return to their home in a beach community and had stopped by for a meal. One of our judges in a bright yellow raincoat was helping three men from the mountains near Boone unload a truck load of food brought in by the Red Cross. Finally, under a tent I saw a school principal and his teacher wife washing the big pots and pans used in meal preparation.

All of this was just confirmation of what I already knew: Ours was a church that did "whatever it takes." Even so, it took us a while to get there.

When Jim Everette joined our staff in 1990, we made a decision as a staff to change his title from minister of education to minister of education and missions. We decided to be "intentional" about engaging our community. As Jim likes to proudly say, "Since that time, there has always been someone on our staff with a title that has something to do with missions."

Jim could bear witness to just how difficult it was to move folks from the pew out into the community. It was not easy work, nor did it happen quickly. When Jim got here, missions meant giving money, studying about mission work, and praying for missionaries. He began to cast a new vision of hands-on ministry in the community. A few people were looking for just such an opportunity. Their stories are told throughout this book.

Jim began to develop those partnerships by getting out and meeting people and learning what their needs were. I asked him to visit the director of every non-profit ministry in town to see what they needed. He got to know them, and they got to know and trust him. Then he brought those needs back to the church.

We began to challenge the church, reminding the people that the church exists primarily for those who are not a part of it. We attempted to create an environment where folks were affirmed that they are gifted; that God desires for them to use their gifts; and that they can do things, big and small, that matter greatly in the kingdom of God. Every time someone asked for a ministry in which they could invest, Jim could match their gifts and talents with someone else's need. He did this with every new member, as well as with long-standing members.

One year when our staff was doing some planning and goal setting, I suggested to Jim that we ought to set a goal of 350 people participating in some kind of mission effort in the coming year. This would have included mission trips, local mission projects, and anything else we did that took them "outside the walls of the church." Jim responded by asking, "What do you want me to do with the other 100?" When I asked what he meant by that, he informed me that we had 450 people already involved that year. Who knew?

Our congregation celebrates all of these ministries. We are excited at what God is doing in and through the people of FBC. And that creates energy for our folks. They've shown a willingness to listen to God's whisper. They've shown a willingness to embrace that which is different from us. They've shown a willingness to be "on mission" for Jesus.

FBC just kept saying "yes" to the opportunities that came our way, and God kept sending opportunities. Not all of our members are involved in everything we do, but everything we do forms the identity of First Baptist and how we see ourselves . . . and how the community sees us, too.

The people in our church (and the people in yours) want to be committed to something larger than themselves. They want to make a difference in the world; and when that is true, when it makes a big difference, they do not resent or resist being asked to make a big commitment. Give them the opportunity.

Cultivating Hopeful Imagination

Pay attention to the Spirit. As you read this story, what did the Spirit prompt in you regarding your own congregation and context?

- Whispers: How is God stirring up your imagination?
- Groans: What needs in your church or community do you think about?
- Praises: What resources or individuals or opportunities come to mind?

Develop missional partnerships. Often, when churches begin to think about reaching out to the community, we decide what we can and will do and then offer it to others. Perhaps we collect food or clothing for area ministries. Or maybe we collect money and give it to an organization. All of these are good and gracious things, and we should continue to do them.

What has made the difference at FBC, though, has been the willingness and the intention to go into the community and say to those on the front lines of ministry: "We are here. We want to help. What do you need?" They may very well need canned food or clothing or money. But they may also need some manpower to fix a fence, or a network of connections in the community to find an apartment for a family in need, or any of a number of other things we could never have thought of but are well resourced to help with.

Such initiative focuses more on the relationship and less on what we think we have to give; it is about building missional partnerships in the community. It says, "We are your neighbor. We are here whenever you need us."

- What missional partnerships do you have in your community?
- What can you do to strengthen some of those relationships?
- To whom do you need to introduce yourself and your church and ask what they need?

Be open to reimagining who you are as a church. When we invited Good Shepherd into our downtown facility, we had just completed a major renovation of the space—new paint, new carpeting, the whole nine yards. Inviting hundreds of homeless men and women to come through our place each week, serving food five days a week in our carpeted fellowship hall, would take a physical toll on that space—a space we were proud of, a space with its fine china in the cabinets that, perhaps, we had too closely identified with who we thought we were as a church.

Saying yes to God often requires us to reimagine ourselves. Saying yes to God asks something of us and challenges who we want to be.

• Are you a "tall steeple church"? A rural congregation? Something in between?
• How does your church's label limit what kind of ministries you think God may want you to be involved in?
• What have you said no to because it might mess up your space?
• What do you wish you could say yes to, but are hesitant because it is outside your comfort zone?

Be the church you dream of being. Only a small percentage of our members actually serve in the ministries for which FBC is best known. But because we tell the stories, we invite the congregation into all of those experiences. Those ministries become our ministries. They shape how we see ourselves, individually and collectively as a congregation, because we are in it together.

We are the church that hosted the soup kitchen, that visits the jail, that partners with the community, that embraces families with special needs, that serves food to hungry folks in front of our church. We are First Baptist Church.

• How would you complete the sentence, "We are the church that . . ."?
• How do you wish that sentence read?
• What do you need to do to make that happen?

Becoming a
Permission-giving Church

You can design your church for growth or for control.
If God inspires a vision for ministry in your people, get out of the way.

> When we allow ministry to bubble up from within the congregation, life can become messy and a bit chaotic. But if we as clergy can sum up enough courage to release our grip on control and get out of the way, the creativity of God and God's people will manifest itself in ways among us that we never thought possible.

"When are we going to start doing some of this stuff?" That was the question posed by a tenth-grade boy to his small group leader Gary Harris, a deacon at FBC Wilmington. When Gary asked what the young man meant, the boy went into his spiel about how, in Sunday school and youth group and small group, we always "study" the Bible. He was looking for some action. Gary simply closed his Bible and asked, "Okay, what do you all want to do?"

Gary is one of a host of small group leaders who meet each week for prayer and Bible study with each grade of boys and girls in our youth group. That year, 2002, Gary's group consisted of five tenth-grade boys. They decided they wanted to go out and do random acts of kindness, so they made a big list of ideas and narrowed it down to a few possibilities. One of the boys, a member at another church who attended our youth group, told them that his dad owned a bottled water distribution company and that there were cases of bottled water in his garage. Maybe they could get some and pass them out to runners or folks playing basketball in the park.

So it began. Gary loaded the boys in his pick-up truck, drove by the young man's garage, and "stole" three cases of bottled water. The boy assured them it would be okay with his dad. Once at the park, one of the boys asked what he should say to strangers when he offered them water. Gary told them to tell the truth. Just say, "I am a part of the youth group

at First Baptist Church, and our small group is out this evening practicing random acts of kindness." And so they did. They had a blast.

The next Tuesday evening, Gary cut short the Bible study and
asked the boys what they wanted to do that week. One of the boys said he
knew a lady at the Krispy Kreme donut shop who would give them some
donuts at a big discount. After acquiring ten dozen donuts, Gary drove
the boys to the New Hanover Regional Medical Center, our local hospital. The boys quickly fanned out on the different floors offering donuts
to nurses, patients, visitors, and anyone else they came upon. They were
not quite so welcomed on the cardiac care floor with Krispy Kremes, but
their efforts seemed to be enjoyed by everyone.

When the weather started to get cold, the guys decided to pass out
hot chocolate to folks waiting in line to enter the St. James night shelter. In the days before Good Shepherd got its new facility, leaders at St.
James Episcopal Church, located one block from FBC, had opened their
basement as a night shelter during the five coldest months of the year.
At the very least, folks off the street had a warm place to sleep. Gary had
volunteered there before, as had one of the boys and his dad, spending
the night with the guests in the basement of the downtown church. The
line formed at 7 p.m., but the doors didn't open until 8 p.m. And it was
cold outside. So the boys came every Tuesday night for weeks, offering a
warm cup of hot chocolate and a friendly face.

Often times, as the folks rolled into the shelter, many of them asked
if anyone had something to eat. The boys wondered how they could meet
this need. Donuts wouldn't cut it for this crowd. Gary suggested that they
go to the store for sandwich supplies. They came back to our activities
center kitchen and made a bunch of peanut butter and jelly sandwiches,
wrapped them in wax paper, and piled into Gary's truck along with some
bags of potato chips. On the way downtown to St. James, they stopped
by the garage for a few more cases of water.

On that cold winter Tuesday night on Market Street in downtown
Wilmington, a group of fifteen-year-old boys passed out PB&J sandwiches, potato chips, and water to hungry homeless people. The Tuesday
night dinner ministry had officially begun. A few weeks later the guys
decided that hot dogs were about as cheap as peanut butter and jelly, so
they started alternating their "menu" each week between the two.

"For a long time that's how we rolled," Gary said, "hot dogs one
week and peanut butter and jelly the next."

As time went on, more kids from our youth group started helping and some key adults started working with them. An organic thing happened: Word of mouth got people to come on Tuesday nights and help prepare and pass out food. Some people came with their kids who were in the youth group; some people came from other churches.

When the winter was over and the shelter closed for the warmer months, hungry folks continued to arrive at 7 o'clock on Tuesday evenings in the hope of receiving food. Hunger was not seasonal, the boys decided, and the dinner ministry became a year-round endeavor. Hundreds more Tuesday nights and thousands more meals would follow.

"Since the first night we handed out hot chocolate almost twelve years ago, there hasn't been a Tuesday night when First Baptist as a church hasn't been out there handing out food to people who walk up," said Gary Harris. "That's one of the things I'm proudest of."

That includes Christmas, Christmas Eve, whatever. Twelve years! Those teenage boys are grown and gone now, but their ministry lives on. Every Tuesday night a kitchen full of youth, college students, and adults prepare a hot meal for anyone in need. Like all ministries, it has evolved.

Eventually someone complained to the city that we were distributing food on the sidewalk, which was city property. The city required that the church apply for a permit each week or the ministry would have to stop—an administrative headache, to be sure. We came up with a better idea. We simply brought the ministry back across the street to our place. Today the Tuesday night meal is served in the First Baptist courtyard on our own church property—with no permit needed.

The St. James shelter has since closed with the opening of the Good Shepherd facility, but there are still plenty of hungry folks living on the streets and under the bridges in downtown Wilmington, so the Tuesday night dinner ministry has continued. Today we serve about fifty people in front of the church and another fifty at nearby Mercy House, a men's shelter. The kids come and go, but the one constant is Gary. He has been the driving force and also a magnet to draw others into what has become a signature ministry of FBC.

Amazingly, some other churches and ministries have taken other nights of the week to replicate what happens at FBC on Tuesdays.

Every year on Super Bowl Sunday and the night of the NCAA national championship basketball game, under Gary's leadership, we open our Fireside Hall downtown for a party to watch the game. The same crowd that comes on Tuesday nights comes on those special nights. Grilled meat, pizza, snacks, dips, soft drinks, desserts, and everything else you would find at such a party in your own home is spread across a couple of tables. A big-screen TV is wheeled in for the game and all the festivities. How cool is that?

One Thursday afternoon, Gary called me with a problem. One of our members, Dennis, had called Gary with an offer of free food. Dennis worked at a large meat packing firm in another town. They had some fresh pork that could not be shipped by their normal means and standards. The food was fine, but it needed to be used immediately or frozen. Dennis said he had a pallet of pork that totaled about 1,000 pounds. Gary wanted to know what to do. I told him to accept it. We could put some of it in our freezers at both the church and our activities center, but he probably needed to call around to see if some church folks might have extra space in their home freezers as well.

About two hours later Gary called again. With a bit more urgency in his voice, he said the pork had arrived—all eight pallets! Four tons of pork needed a home. Once again God was ahead of us on this one. Within another two hours Gary had every box of pork in a freezer somewhere in Wilmington. For the next several months the Tuesday Night meal took on a whole new vibe.

Twig, another deacon who helped on Tuesdays, loves to cook—anything and everywhere. Cooking is his passion. He hauled his huge BBQ grill into the back parking lot at the church on Tuesday nights and began cooking up our newly acquired bounty. Roast pork loin, barbecued ribs, and grilled pork chops made the weekly menu look like it came straight from one of the finer restaurants in town. This is what happens when people's passions are matched with the needs of others.

On the Tuesday night before the ribbon cutting marking the opening of the new overnight shelter that would cause the old St. James Shelter to close, Gary and the other missionaries who joined him in providing food for the guests who frequented the shelter wondered whether they should continue providing this ministry. Many of the people they had been serving would be relocating from downtown Wilmington to the neighborhood of the new shelter that is more than a mile away. They had begun praying about what to do.

That night, while they were serving dinner on the plaza, a luxury automobile stopped and parked across the street. After a few minutes the window rolled down and Gary noticed a hand beckoning him to the car. When he got across the street, he found two well-dressed women in the car. One of them asked what they were doing each Tuesday. Gary explained the ministry and that it was essentially the work of our youth. The other lady reached across and handed Gary a rolled-up bundle of cash.

"Keep doing what you are doing," she said.

Gary put the cash in his pocket, thanked the women, and headed back across the street. One of the men who was helping serve that evening asked Gary how much they gave him. Gary didn't know. You don't take out a wad of cash like that and count it on the streets of downtown. When they went back inside, they counted it: more than $900.

That story of provision and confirmation continues to repeat itself. Whether it is a corporation or a stranger in a passing car, people keep investing in this simple feeding ministry started by a handful of kids who wanted to do the "stuff" that Jesus and the Bible teach us to do.

Much like our jail ministry, only a small percentage of our FBC folks participate in the Tuesday night ministry, but everyone knows that we are the church that feeds hungry people downtown on Tuesday nights. This is a ministry that has woven itself into the very fabric of the congregation. One mother of two teens told me that on the rare occasions when she needed to punish one of them, nothing much seemed to get their attention. No TV, no problem. No Internet, so what. Grounded, no big deal. But if she said "no Tuesday night feeding," that got their attention.

On a Tuesday night in late August of 2013, my wife and I stopped by just to say hello to the group and to see who was there. Nearly a dozen of the more than thirty folks working that night were college students. All of them were headed out the next week to return to their colleges. They wanted one more night of cooking and serving before they left. On that same evening one of the workers was a church member who used to be a guest on the street himself. Now he was cooking for others.

Out in the courtyard the kids do all the serving. Some of the regular guests have learned their names, and in turn the youth have learned their names. There is an odd sense of community that emerges when everyone—our guests and our youth and adults—is sitting on the low wall around the courtyard sharing a meal together. When one of the guests wondered aloud who I was, one of the youth told him that I was the former pastor. He made his way to where I sitting and introduced himself. He just wanted to say thank you for what our church was doing on Tuesday nights. One of the leaders had challenged the kids "to see Jesus in the face of every person they served." That night I think I did.

"We just make it a point to be there with a smile and as much food as we can," Gary says. "Sometimes it's a wonderful experience, like tonight. We passed out our last sandwich to the last person who walked up. When things happen like that, when it's nothing you did or could have planned, it's an amazing thing." That's a God thing, for sure.

Jesus said, "I was hungry and you fed me." If hunger was a problem in Jesus' time, you would think we might have overcome that by now. You think about all the food that is thrown out of homes and restaurants every day, but there are still folks who do not have enough to eat. As long as there are hungry people, the church has a ministry to them—not only to their bellies, but also to their souls.

The most wonderful thing about our Tuesday night ministry is that the staff had nothing to do with it. It is one of the many ministries at FBC that has "bubbled up" from among our people.

Being a Missional Church

Ever since Jim Everette's title changed to minister of education and mission, expressing the desire of our church to move in a new direction, being "on mission" has become part of the core identity of FBC—for the congregation as a whole and for each person in it. Jim's philosophy of mission is pretty simple: Love others as Jesus loves you. That's what we try to do. We don't always get it done or do it perfectly, but we try.

While being a missional church may mean different things to different people, there are four important components to being a missional church that Jim has elevated for us at FBC:

1. Missional churches do not exist without mission-minded, visionary leaders. Such leadership doesn't come just from the pulpit; it also comes from the pew. While the pastoral leaders in our congregation attempt to be visionary and to lead those in our congregation to exercise their spiritual gifts, and sometimes to stretch beyond their comfort zones to live out Christ's command to go into all the world and tell the good news, we are constantly entertaining ideas and suggestions about ministry possibilities that come from the pew.

2. Each of us is called by God to be God's people, commissioned by Jesus to be the presence of Christ in all we are and all we do, everywhere we go. As a congregation, we are constantly praying that God will open our eyes to those in need around us and also give us the boldness to act on those opportunities. We prepare to say yes. We don't have a cold water committee that douses new ideas.

3. Being missional is a mindset and an attitude, not a program. We don't have a missions program. We have ongoing mission projects and missional opportunities. We equip people to serve as missionaries. Sometimes that includes studies and training. Oftentimes it means sending folks out on mission and walking with them along the way. We used to have a business conference every quarter; we don't anymore. We have missional celebrations. We've embraced the reality that the primary business of the church is to be on mission with Jesus. So instead of having a business conference, it's always a missional celebration. We celebrate what God is doing in us and through us.

4. Being missional is organic. We let ministries bubble up and arise from within the congregation through the gifts God has given. We are a permission-giving church. We believe in the power of the Holy Spirit to work, not only through the staff of the church, but also through the congregation. When ministries bubble up from in and among our folks, we provide resources and encouragement and get out of the way and let God do what God wants to do.

I'll never forget the day Jayne came to ask about a group of women desiring to start a prayer shawl ministry. They wanted to meet each week at our activities center to knit prayer shawls and take them to people in the hospital. I must admit that in the beginning I felt like the whole thing was a bit hokey. But it seemed otherwise harmless. Ladies knitting and praying for others . . . How bad could that be?

One morning I stopped by the hospital early to pray with a woman who was having knee replacement surgery that day. On the way home that evening I stopped in again to see how she was doing. When I entered her room, I saw that her knee was in one of those contraptions that flexes the knee back and forth, often with some measure of pain. Wrapped around her knee was one of the prayer shawls. She quickly pointed it out to me and said: "You know, Mike, I did not know we had this kind of ministry at First Baptist. But let me tell you what it has meant to me today. Connie (one of the ladies in the ministry) brought it to me, and she told me they had prayed over the shawl and for me this morning. She said they brought it as a reminder that my church was remembering me in prayer until I was able to be up and on my own. How wonderful is that?"

A few weeks later another member, Tom, had to have a portion of his leg amputated. Having had prayer with him and his sons the morning of the surgery, I stopped by the hospital that evening to check on his progress and his spirits. He was a bit philosophical about the whole ordeal, but then he threw back the bed covers to show me the stump of his leg—proudly wrapped in a prayer shawl delivered that afternoon by one of the women. He told her to just "leave it in the window," which she did before she left and after promising to remember him in prayer. Later that evening he had asked a nurse to give him the bag with the shawl. He then asked her to help him wrap it around his leg. He said, "Mike, in some odd way, that thing gives me comfort. I'm going to be okay."

Apparently the prayer shawl ministry was having an impact, but it did not stop there. As Jim Everette likes to say, "Elevate what you want people to imitate." We do that best by telling stories.

From time to time in our worship services, we ask someone to share a story of what God is doing in their ministry. In one of these "mission moments" at FBC, two of the women who lead the prayer shawl ministry came forward to tell the story of why they do what they do and ways that God's grace and peace have blessed many of our home-bound and hospitalized members.

On that particular Sunday, a children's sermon was to follow the mission moment, so, as the women were sharing about the prayer shawl ministry, a couple dozen preschool and elementary-aged children were gathered at the platform behind them.

We are always challenging everyone in the congregation to find their own ministry. We ask the questions over and over again: How has God gifted you? What is God calling you to do in our church or in the community?

A ten-year-old girl came up to Jeannie Troutman, our minister to children, after that worship service. She told Jeannie that she had been praying about finding a ministry and had been wondering if God could use her love of sewing to bless other people. When she heard the women talk about the prayer shawl ministry, she felt like God was talking to her. She didn't know how to knit, but she was sure she could learn.

"There's one big problem, though," she said. "The prayer shawl ministry meets on Tuesday mornings at eleven o'clock. I don't think I'll be able to make the meetings. I kind of have to go to school."

Jeannie assured her that the women would love to teach her how to knit and that she could work on her prayer shawls at home. She affirmed the young girl for paying attention to how God might want to use the things she already loves to do to touch other people with his love.

When a ten-year-old girl gets it, you know that being "on mission" is becoming a part of your church's DNA.

Two months after I retired as pastor at FBC, I was diagnosed with prostate cancer. Two months later I had surgery. All of a sudden, I got a prayer shawl of my own. Knit in "old gold and black," the colors of my beloved alma mater Wake Forest University, my shawl came with the same letter sent to each recipient. It read as follows:

Dear Mike,

This prayer shawl was knit especially for you with love. May this prayer shawl warm and comfort you when you are weak and weary. Whenever you wear it, know that God's love is woven into every stitch; and if you would like, pray this prayer:

Dear Heavenly Father, you formed my being. You knit me together in my mother's womb. To my flesh and blood you gave me the breath of life. O Loving God, renew me this day in your love. Grant me hope to sustain me, and may this prayer shawl be for me a sign of your presence. May it . . . warm me when I am weary, surround me with comfort, and encircle me with your healing touch. Oh, Jesus Christ, you who healed the broken in body and spirit, be with me and with all who suffer this day. Thank you, Lord, for your many blessings. Amen.

God loves you, and so do we . . .
First Baptist Church Prayer Shawl Ministry

It is not the job of the church staff to filter out what God might want to do. The ministry that God is bringing forth may ultimately look far different than when it first bubbles up, but you have to take that first step to find out.

Who knew that allowing teenage boys to hand out water bottles in the park one night would turn into an enduring ministry with hungry and homeless people in our community?

Who knew that blessing a few women with a passion for knitting would turn into a significant part of the pastoral care of our congregation?

Truth be told, the staff is just not that smart. We may very well have overlooked both of those ministries in their early days had there not been lay people with passion and a sense of calling giving leadership to them. Ministry based on the gifts and callings of the congregation cannot be a top-down endeavor. It must be both top down and bottom up. If not, we will miss much of what God wants to do through us and among us.

We believe that God has a plan for First Baptist Church. Parts of that plan he reveals to the staff. We believe that if God brings the ministry, God will raise up folks—members or new folks—with the gifts and passions necessary to accomplish what he has shown us he wants to do.

We also believe that God reveals parts of his plan to us through our people. Our job is to pay attention to what God is doing in people and in the congregation through people. If God's vision is bubbling up in the people, we need to start the ministry.

Both scenarios are God at work, showing us where he wants to take his church.

Cultivating Hopeful Imagination

Pay attention to the Spirit. As you read this story, what did the Spirit prompt in you regarding your own congregation and context?

• Whispers: How is God stirring up your imagination?
• Groans: What needs in your church or community do you think about?
• Praises: What resources or individuals or opportunities come to mind?

Be open to the movement of the Spirit. One of the most important lessons we have learned over the years is that you can't institutionalize the movement of God's Spirit. It doesn't move at a set time through certain persons or specific committees. It moves when and where it wills.

That can be intimidating. Our staff is as prone to want to control things as much as anyone else. Let's face it, we like to keep a handle on what's going on in our churches. That's part of our responsibility, isn't it? It's certainly neater that way.

More often than not, though, such need to control is driven by fear. God has always had to tell those he has chosen to lead, "Do not be afraid." We are no different.

If God's vision is bubbling up in the people, start the ministry. Not everything that bubbles up comes to fruition. We are simply learning to get out of the way and give something a chance to happen.

By the same token, it is not the job of staff to make everyone else's visions happen. If ministry bubbles up from among our people, we are not called to take it and lead it but to act as equippers and encouragers. If the one with the vision does not have the will or the desire to take hold of what God has brought forth, then it is probably a sign that the timing for that ministry is not quite right.

The ministry that God is bringing forth may ultimately look far different than when it first bubbles up. If we squelch it too soon, though, we will never know what it might have become.

- Where is God's Spirit bubbling up in your congregation?
- How can you equip and encourage those with that emerging vision?
- What squelches the work of God's Spirit in your people?
- How can you create a climate of expectation that pays attention to how God might be at work among you?
- What do you need to do differently?

Create a culture of calling. "Elevate what you want people to imitate." Those words have served us well over the years as we have tried to be intentional about creating a culture of calling at FBC. The telling of stories has been a key component in that effort.

Mike and Jim have always done a great job of weaving in stories from the pulpit of folks finding a place of ministry. I remember those stories creating a sense of anticipation and expectation in me as a new member of FBC for what my own ministry might look like.

About a year after I joined FBC, Mike told the story to our congregation of David Washburn, a young man who had felt the call to go to seminary. It was more than just an announcement. We as a congregation were being invited into his story. We were a part of making it happen, Mike said, implying that we also now had a stake in watching this calling unfold in the years ahead. David's story was now part of our story as a congregation.

The next year, two more guys responded to God's call to ministry. I went to divinity school the year after that, along with three other members of FBC. Telling the story of David and the others who followed him into ministry did not create God's call in me, but it gave me a picture of what it might look like to respond to what I already knew God wanted me to do—and permission and courage to do it. In all, eleven folks from FBC entered divinity school over a ten-year period.

The folks in our congregations need that picture of what responding to a call to ministry looks like, whether that is vocational ministry or feeding hungry people or knitting prayer shawls. Sometimes we forget how scary it can be to say yes to God.

• What stories do you tell to your congregation?
• What message do the stories convey?
• What do you elevate that you want people to imitate?

The Means to an End

Don't invest yourself in surface change.
Look for God's transforming vision.

> We talk a lot about buildings at First Baptist Church Wilmington, and
> we have a lot to talk about. Conventional wisdom in the twenty-first
> century says churches ought to divest themselves of brick-and-mortar
> structures. They are too costly to maintain, and they are almost always
> the least-used space in town. This is often true. But at FBC we sought
> to acquire adjacent space to accommodate our growth and to serve
> the various ministries of the church. We believe God was a part of
> that from the beginning, but only so long as we did not let buildings
> become an end themselves but rather a means to more worthy ends.

In the mid-1990s, First Baptist Wilmington was truly struggling for
space to meet the needs of the growing congregation. Across a small
alley from the church sat the majestic WLI Building, a place with
a unique history. It had originally been the home of John A. Taylor. A
wealthy merchant/trader, he built the home in the mid 1850s for his
family. It consisted of a basement that housed the kitchen and servants
quarters, a main floor that included the dining room and other formal
areas, and sleeping quarters on the third floor. All twelve rooms were
heated by fireplaces. Atop the home was a "widow's walk," a small room
that looked out on the river.

By the latter part of the nineteenth century, the home had become
the headquarters of the Wilmington Light Infantry (WLI). That was in
the day when individual towns and counties formed their own militias.
In a mix of legend and historical fact, the WLI played a significant role in
the only *coup d'état* ever to occur on American soil.

During Reconstruction in the post-Civil War South, blacks often
held significant elected positions in local governments. Wilmington was
no different. In November 1898, some of the leading white citizens of
Wilmington decided to put an end to that level of participation. The

local black newspaper was burned and the editor run out of town. The WLI took its Gatling gun into the streets of the Brooklyn neighborhood and killed a large number of blacks. The number remains in dispute.

The whites said no more than seven were killed, while the blacks said the number was greater than 300. It is assumed that the truth lies somewhere in between. A now-deceased member of our congregation, Wallace West, recalled his grandfather as saying that he went to the sight of the massacre and saw people piling dozens of bodies into wagons to be carried away. The net result was that all of the black elected officials were forced to resign from office to be replaced by whites. It was truly one of Wilmington's darkest days.

So, this WLI building had been a home for a family and an armory for a military unit. During World War I all these local units were organized into the United States Army and into reserve or national guard units. The vestiges of the WLI became a sort of veterans organization. The basement level provided a place for them to meet, smoke cigars, and drink. They had personal lockers where they kept their spirits and personal effects. It was in effect a private club for veterans.

Right after World War II the WLI group gave the building to New Hanover County to serve as the county library. The WLI retained rights to the basement space, while the county took over the upper floors. The county then added three floors to the back of the building to serve as the "stacks" for the book collection. The county also built a couple of wing offices on the sides to the rear of the building. The impressive granite front remained intact. For more than twenty-five years the WLI served as the county library.

Somewhere about 1975, the library relocated to an old abandoned department store location downtown and the building was sold to the City of Wilmington for its building permit and code enforcement offices. Twenty years later those offices relocated and the city had no use for the WLI building. It sat empty, except for a handful of WLI members who still made their way downtown to the "club" once a month. Desperate for space and parking, we contacted the city about the possibility of purchasing the WLI.

The city manager said the leadership would entertain bids, but because it was a public building, it would be subject to the upset bid process required by North Carolina law. Since it was right across the street from the New Hanover County courthouse, we knew that attorneys would be willing to pay top dollar for such a prime location. While we were willing to pay a fair price, we did not want to engage in a bidding war. I asked the county manager if there was any other way to proceed. She said if the church owned property that the city needed, we could trade property and avoid the bid process.

When I told her we did not own any land elsewhere, she noted that the city needed land for two new fire stations. If the Baptist church could purchase those parcels, then perhaps we could, after proper appraisals were done, work out an exchange. She suggested that we meet with the fire chief to see where he needed land.

We sent one of our deacons, Carlton Fisher, who was a real estate broker and developer, to meet with the fire chief. When the chief spread out the maps, he indicated two sites marked in red where he wanted to build new fire stations. Carlton asked how close the sites needed to be in relation to the red dots. One mile? A half mile? The chief said, "No, we want those two parcels that are marked."

When Carlton came back to me, he was a bit defeated. He said he doubted that either of those parcels would ever be for sale. One was owned by a large commercial developer, and while it was an odd-shaped triangular piece of property, it was in a prime location on a major roadway. The second was owned by a company in another town, and was probably reserved to expand its growing business. Carlton was convinced that neither owner would give up such valuable property.

This is where the praying and miracle part of the story begin. We had not yet taken all of this to the entire church because there were so many moving parts and so much uncertainty. But our trustees and a handful of other leaders had been brought in to see if we might fashion a deal we could then take to the congregation. But we asked that tight little group of eight or ten to pray each day and to make that prayer a priority. We needed the WLI building, and we were going to need the Lord's help if it was to be.

Although I had conducted the funeral of the father of the developer, I had no relationship with him nor did he have a relationship to the church. We approached him about the parcel, and he gave us a price on it that was at least double the going rate. He was asking more than what the city would have required for the WLI building and parking lot in downtown. In other words, it was outrageous. We assumed that we were "dead in the water" on that one.

Oddly enough, I recalled that a young man in our church worked for the company that owned the other parcel—the one being held for future expansion. I called and told him what we needed to do and to see if he would talk to the owners about selling the property to the church. He laughed. It was his opinion that there was no way that would happen. I begged him to ask, and volunteered to go make an appeal in person in the town where the owners lived. But he wanted to talk to them first on his own.

A couple of days later, this man called to say that the owners would sell the parcel to the church, and the price was imminently fair. He was surprised, and we were elated. We signed an option to purchase that property, but we were only halfway home.

Carlton went back to the fire chief inquiring about a bit of flexibility on the other site. There was none according to the chief. It was the one parcel still undeveloped in the fastest growing part of town. He had to have that particular spot. The developer would not budge on price. The chief would not budge on location.

One evening I had just come out of a meeting with this group at our activities center. We had spent several hours trying to devise a strategy that might yield the needed result. We left our meeting more than discouraged. In the hallway were some members of another church committee/team that had just concluded their meeting also. One of our deacons, who was a part of the other group, asked what our group was meeting about. While our deacons did not know any details, they did know we were talking with the city about the WLI.

As I related to him our dilemma, he casually asked exactly where the piece of property was that we needed. As I explained it to him, he said, "Are you talking about that little triangular piece right near [such and such place]?" I said, "Yes, what do you know about it?"

He went on to tell me that he thought the company he worked for actually had an option on that little piece of property. I could not believe my ears. It was by now 10 p.m., but since the owner of his company was leaving on a trip out of the country the next morning, our deacon called him then and there. He did indeed have an option on the property that was set to expire at the end of the month. He asked to speak to me and peppered me with several questions. He could not believe what the developer was asking us for the parcel. His option was for an amount less than half of the new asking price. In the end he said, "Mike, don't worry about this. We will handle it when I get home." And he did. He exercised his option on the last day he could and bought the parcel, much to the chagrin of the developer. He, in turn, sold it to the church for the price he paid for it.

Two unique and individual pieces of property desperately needed by the city for fire stations, two men in our church who did not own the parcels but who worked for companies that did, two business owners willing to sell those parcels at very reasonable prices to the church . . .

We at First Baptist talk a lot about the unseen hand of God at work in our lives and in the life of this congregation. This story is just one more example among dozens of others of God at work. There was a time in my life when I would have chalked all of this up to coincidence, but not anymore. Church leaders and staff alike have come to a place where we simply stand in wonder and awe of the things God does in our midst.

Of course, it was not to be all that easy. Once the word got out that the city was making this exchange deal with the church, the whole reality of "principalities and powers" broke out in the newspapers and on the television and talk radio. The attacks on the church and the city were relentless.

The first hurdle had been long anticipated. The WLI club members were incensed that the city was doing this. They feared that the Baptists would kick them out or, absent that, not let them keep their "lockers" in the basement. As a part of our agreement, before things became public, we agreed that they could maintain that space as long as there was any one of them living who wanted to make use of the basement space. In other words, nothing in their agreement with the county or city changed when the church got involved.

But still there was outrage. It was an affront to every veteran who had ever served in any branch of the military. The city had no business doing business with a church. If the church owns it, it will lose its historical significance. People piled into city council meetings. The men of the WLI, all of them over the age of eighty at the time and many of them on walkers or canes, showed up at the council meeting to protest. They hired a fiery lawyer to represent them in this seeming injustice.

When it came time for someone from the church to speak, it was the chair of our trustees who spoke, and who was also the next-door neighbor and best friend of the fiery lawyer. They even rode to the council meeting together. He stood and calmly explained that the church had provided a great service to the city in procuring the two needed sites for the new fire houses. Costly legal battles over the rights of eminent domain were avoided. Further, he reminded them that not only did the church intend to allow the WLI group to maintain meeting space, but we also intended to keep the name WLI (and all the attendant memorial plaques) on the building.

The vote was unanimous. The council was grateful. And in the end, the WLI gentlemen were quite pleased. When their numbers got down to only seven of them still living, they gave up the keys and the rights to the building. They thanked us for keeping our word.

Today the WLI houses our church offices, chapel, several youth and adult Sunday school spaces, a room for our special needs children, and shower and toilet facilities for hosting the Wilmington Interfaith Hospitality Network families who are temporarily homeless. It also allowed us to convert our former office space into much needed Sunday school space.

We petitioned the city to close the little alley between the WLI and the main church facility. When that request was approved, we built a two-story connector building in the old alley that allowed us to meet three significant needs: additional rest room space, a large gathering foyer on both floors, and a focal entrance from a new and beautiful courtyard and columbarium in the front center of the church. And we got another dozen parking spaces in the process.

Lest that all sound like a bricks-and-mortar story, know this: Everything about this story strengthened the church. We learned about leaning on God. We learned a lot about the need to do all the little things we needed to do. We learned the importance of keeping our promises. We learned not to get too discouraged when things did not go exactly as we had planned. We learned that more space gave us more options for ministry. We learned that when we invited people and ministries into our house, it always blessed us more than it did them.

It was not just bricks and mortar. It was what those bricks allowed us to do in the name of Jesus Christ—just another miracle in the life of the church.

Transforming Lives, Brick by Brick

A tiny parking lot 40 feet across was all that separated the New Hanover County Law Enforcement Center (jail) from the First Baptist Church. Together they occupied a full city block in downtown Wilmington. The jail was only 27 years old, while the church house was 140 years old. For nearly three decades, the two buildings peacefully coexisted as benevolent strangers, but they were soon to become unlikely siblings in a unique, blended family of faith and purpose.

Jails are unique properties, and this one was worn out. It had been used 24 hours a day 365 days a year. With 500 inmates, the facility served 1,500 meals a day from a rather small kitchen. Toilets flushing and showers taken put a strain on the plumbing system, too. And that was only half of the building.

The other half housed the administrative offices of the sheriff's department, the 911 emergency call center, and the emergency management offices—which since we live in "hurricane alley" was fairly significant. That side of the building had a few more windows and was essentially comprised of office space. But it leaked badly. For years we had heard about the leaks and the generally poor condition of the building on the administrative side.

One day after getting out of my car in the church parking lot, I looked up on the roof of the jail to see the county manager and another gentleman walking along the parapet wall. When I called up to ask what they were doing, the manager said, "Trying to figure out how to stop these leaks." "Good luck" was all I could offer in response.

North Carolina law instructs the grand jury of the court system to conduct a tour of the county jail at least once annually to make sure that inmates are cared for appropriately and that the building is safe and clean. The only time I had been "inside" the cell blocks was when I served on a grand jury. It was a jail, spartan in every way. It was clean, and the inmates seemed to be okay with their treatment in the jail. But it was very crowded, with several inmates sleeping on mattresses on the floor.

Some watchdog group that pays attention to such matters a few years later threatened a lawsuit against the county for overcrowding at the jail. Given the confined space of the old jail, architects looked at several options to solve the space problems. None was readily available or affordable. So the county commissioners determined to construct a new modern jail eleven miles from downtown. That decision in and of itself created some controversy. The public wants offenders put in jail, but we do not enjoy having to pay for it.

The question before the commissioners was what to do with an old jail that was essentially "worn out." Since the county was desperately in need of more office space, they looked at what it would take to fix the building. One architect's estimate was $4 million plus. The county finally opted to buy and up-fit an old shopping center more in the center of the county that had ample parking for the offices of county government. And after the move to the new jail, the old one sat empty.

It was then that we inquired of the commissioners if they would be interested in selling the jail to the church. We had made the assumption that we would most likely have to tear down the building while hoping to save the two-story underground parking deck with space for eighty cars. For a church with less than thirty parking places, this would have been a godsend.

Most of that whole story is detailed in the first chapter about Ms. Evelina. But once the politics played out and we had a contract with the county, it was time to do our "due diligence." How much would it take to fix the leaks? Is the building structurally sound? Do the HVAC and plumbing and electrical systems work? How will we pay for it? And of course, the congregation would want to know how we planned to make use of an old jail.

Right from the beginning, mostly I suspect in reaction to media reports, we had members speaking out against the purchase. Two families announced their intentions to leave the church since our plans—of which there were none at the time—would cause the deterioration of the historic downtown. It was exhilarating and disappointing all at the same time. Both our faith and our motives were questioned publically. We could not say that we had not been warned.

Dan Southerland at Flamingo Road had told us that "when you begin to do God's work, the devil will attack from every corner." Doug Bailey of the Center for Urban Ministry warned us that "as you move forward, you will become all too well acquainted with the principalities and powers of which the scriptures speak."

The original vision of salvaging the parking decks gave way to one far more noble, and hopefully, Christ-like. What if we could create a center for non-profit ministries that provided space at below-market rates? Non-profits struggle to be efficient with limited funds available. With that rather undefined and murky vision, we began to pursue the other issues.

Being a rather large church has several advantages, not the least of which is a group of contractors and engineers whose expertise helped us greatly in this process. Structurally, the jail was a fortress. The systems were old and had some issues, but they were serviceable. At first, though, no one could get a handle on the leaks. After some investigative work by our engineers and contractors, they came up with actions that they were certain would solve the problem.

It was no wonder that the building leaked. The original windows had been put in backwards with flashings improperly installed. Over time, that simply invited water "into" the building. The other design flaw in the jail was the brick parapet that ran around the top sides of the flat-roofed structure. Replacing all the windows in the administrative side and putting a metal cap on the parapets eliminated all the leaks. That was not a cheap process, but the repair costs were folded into a capital campaign that was already underway at the church. The building was dry. We had our parking. Now the hard work was about to begin. We had not done a market study on the needs of non-profits, but we still believed there was a need.

During our time of due diligence we created four teams for that purpose. Each team was chaired by one of the three men who had worked with me on securing the jail from the beginning. Claude Arnold chaired the mission team charged with charting the course for how we might use the building. Carlton Fisher led the structural team to determine what repairs might be needed and how all the internal systems were functioning. Berry Trice led the finance team looking for ways to pay for or finance the project. Jim Everette led an administrative team dealing with day-to-day issues. Another twenty members of the congregation served on these various teams.

As work on the building began, it soon became obvious that we needed someone to manage this thing we had created. Joe Capell had recently moved back to Wilmington to retire at the beach. He and his wife had joined FBC and had become very active in the life and ministry of the church. When I called to ask if he would be interested in a "part time" job as executive director, he agreed to listen to me and to pray about it with his wife Mararuth. When Joe said "yes," he got more than he bargained for. So did we. Joe was amazing.

One of the great challenges we faced was that of bringing the building up to code. Add to that the fact that the building was heated and cooled by a "closed loop" system tied into the county courthouse across the street, and you can see how complex things had gotten for the new owners of an old jail. The systems had to be disconnected and downsized. Every day seemed to bring new challenges. Graffiti had to be removed from walls in the parking deck. The walls of the jail also held some amazing artwork—some of it profane, other parts of it profound. From images of Marilyn Monroe to Christ on the cross, from the American eagle to praying hands, from Bible verses to the vilest profanities, those walls told dozens of stories.

A lot of problems got solved because people came to us to be a part of what we were trying to do. Landscaping in the courtyard was accomplished through a Boy Scout Eagle project. A huge, nearly-new hot water heater was donated by a motel that was being torn down. Miracles seemed to happen every week to offset our challenges.

Joe pulled together groups of volunteers from the church for all kinds of work inside and outside of the building. He recruited ministry partners from the community. (We never refer to our partners as tenants; we partner in ministry together.) Joe worked countless more hours than those on his schedule. Middle-of-the-night leaking pipes, problems on his days off, and a whole host of other issues laid claim to Joe's retirement. But he met them all.

We had also formed a separate 501(c)3 corporation with its own board of directors to run what was to be called the Jo Ann Carter Harrelson Center. The board members gave oversight to Joe, and he kept them in the loop on all developments. There were leases to be negotiated and signed. There were spaces to be renovated. There were civic clubs and churches that needed to hear the story of the Harrelson Center. The board did its part and then some, but it was Joe who carried the load.

The day we dedicated the Harrelson Center was beautiful. Joe and his crew of volunteers had set up a spread of food worthy of a big hotel caterer. For Bobby Harrelson and his daughters and their families, it was a day that honored his late wife whose dream it was to see the center become what it was becoming. Jo Ann's siblings were present along with local elected officials and some of Bobby's closest friends from around North and South Carolina. Of course, many in the church family and all of our new partners were there also. It was nothing short of a grand celebration.

Partners in the Harrelson Center include Cape Fear Habitat for Humanity and Wilmington Area Rebuilding Ministry (WARM), both ministries that seek to put an end to substandard housing in our area. The Cape Fear Housing Land Trust provides innovative stewardship of land to create opportunities for home ownership. Another partner is Communities in Schools of Cape Fear (CISCF). Housed at the

Harrelson Center, the Wilmington center for Inspiration, Recreation, and Education (WIRE) after-school program complements CISCF's other programs, working with the public schools and "at risk" students in the area to make sure they continue to make progress toward graduation.

Phoenix Employment Ministry does a fabulous work helping the sheltered homeless and the near homeless to find jobs. Philippians 3 Ministry seeks to rebuild and restore the lives of women torn apart by circumstance by giving them hope through spiritual renewal and direct involvement.

Cape Fear Resource Conservation and Development seeks to improve the social, economic, and environmental quality of life in a five-county area. Centre of Redemption focuses its ministry on the young women who are survivors of sex trafficking to help them recover from the past in order that they might live productive and meaningful lives in the future. Also, the North Carolina courts have a drug treatment and DWI court that seeks to identify and rehabilitate non-violent offenders with substance abuse issues. These administrative offices are housed in the Harrelson Center, and classes for their clients are often held at the church.

Other partners have included the Southeastern Sickle Cell Association, Campus Crusade, Christian Women's Job Corps, Outside the Walls, and Life Builders. One of the payoffs of this kind of eclectic mix is the opportunity for collaboration it creates between our partners.

In a story in the *Wilmington Star-News* (11/4/09), Kitty Yerkes, the resource coordinator for Cape Fear Habitat for Humanity, said, "We love this building. It's downtown, it's accessible, and there is a lot more space. And we have the synergy with other non-profits."

All of the administrative space at the center is now fully leased, but the jail cells sit empty. All of the metal (stainless steel, copper, iron, and such) has been removed and sold for scrap. The original plan was to convert that space into housing for the low-income elderly and/or the developmentally disabled through the use of tax credits. While we spent many hours trying to make that work with the National Development Council in Washington, D.C., the simple fact is that the jail space was not big enough to make such an effort economically viable. How that space is to be used is now the primary focus of the current board.

When Joe Capell retired from the Harrelson Center, the board asked another FBC member, Kerry Taylor, to assume the interim executive director position, which he did quite ably for several months. Finally, the board called another FBC member, Vicki Dull, to take up the leadership role. Just as Joe was the person needed to launch the center, Vicki has proven to be the one taking it to the next level.

Vicki's enthusiasm for the work of the Harrelson Center leaves little doubt that she and the board will continue to fuel a transforming vision for the future of the old jail. At a recent fund-raising luncheon for the Harrelson Center, we heard the story of a woman who showed up at the center with all kinds of needs. The ways in which Vicki, her little staff, and a cadre of friends reached out to help change the trajectory of this woman's life is amazing. A structure that had long been a place of incarceration has been rather miraculously turned into a place of redemption.

The folks at FBC would say all of these stories about the wild set of circumstances for acquiring property were nothing less than the hand of God at work. God gave us what we needed to accomplish that to which we had been called. All of that came to us as encouragement. With great hope and vivid imagination, we found ourselves always looking around the corner for "what next." It has been an incredibly exciting ride.

While a lot of media folk took shots at the church, the county, and the process of acquisition, in the end, and because the church did what it said it would do, those views began to change. An editorial in our local newspaper, titled "Transforming lives, brick by brick," offered in part these words:

> Churches usually stress transformation as part of their mission, and Wilmington's First Baptist Church at Fifth Avenue and Market Street is doing just that. This time, however, the church has saved a building and is hosting community groups that help transform lives.
>
> That bulk of red brick on Princess Street that once housed the New Hanover County jail is now the Jo Ann Carter Harrelson Center, an outreach arm of the church run under a separate foundation.
>
> One of the biggest obstacles for outreach agencies is finding a home. Commercial real estate in Wilmington is obviously not cheap, and groups have been crammed into tight spaces not conducive to their work. Sometimes, related agencies have been housed miles apart, making it even more difficult to serve a population that may have limited transportation . . .

After being a close neighbor to the jail for years, the good folks at First Baptist saw an opportunity for ministry when the jail moved to its new location, near the airport. A generous gift from the Harrelson family allowed the church to purchase the building from the county—for about a sixth of its listed value. The fruits of the project are beginning to be seen.

The symbolism of this particular building from a place of imprisonment to a place of empowerment is certainly compelling. But it is also a reminder of the many outreach groups that do such good work across the entire region.

Whether they be religious or secular, they all deserve a loud amen.

(*Wilmington Star News,* 10/4/08)

Cultivating Hopeful Imagination

Pay attention to the Spirit. As you read this story, what did the Spirit prompt in you regarding your own congregation and context?

• Whispers: How is God stirring up your imagination?
• Groans: What needs in your church or community do you think about?
• Praises: What resources or individuals or opportunities come to mind?

Watch for God at work. We speak a lot about the unseen hand of God. It has been an integral part of our story. There is nothing we can do to create that reality. All we can do is keep our eyes open and believe and watch for God at work.

The hand of God is the only way to explain the circumstance that led to the acquisitions of the WLI building and the NHC Law Enforcement Center. We hold both of these buildings as a holy trust, not ends in themselves, but a means to accomplishing the work of God that would not be possible without them.

• What opportunity has come your way that can only be explained by the unseen hand of God?
• How do you hold that circumstance or resource, and whatever it provided for your congregation, as a holy trust?
• For what greater end might God have given it to you?

Develop far-sighted vision. Buildings are long-term propositions, commitments not to be entered into lightly. Buildings can create as many challenges as they solve problems. But sometimes God calls us to take on a vision for the long haul. There may be nay-sayers along the way. Far-sighted vision can sometimes be misunderstood. But if God is directing the vision, those critics may very well come to see what you are doing in a different way—eventually.

FBC faced much harsh and public criticism as we went about acquiring the WLI building and the NHC Law Enforcement Center, much of it coming from local news editorials in print and on television and talk radio. But eventually, on July 26, 2007, Karl Davis, then the general manager of WECT-TV in Wilmington, offered this word at the close of the evening news that day:

> This commentary is about the old county jail on Market Street in downtown Wilmington and vision. You see, some people are near-sighted. Those are the people who operate out of fear and are opposed to everything. In this case, the near-sighted people complained that the county sold the building too cheap and they feared the building would become a homeless shelter.
>
> Then there are the far-sighted people, the ones with vision like Pastor Michael Queen and the parishioners of First Baptist Church. At first, they didn't know exactly what this building would become, but they knew it could make a difference in people's lives in a positive way.
>
> Through a generous gift from Bobby Harrelson in memory of his wife, Jo Ann, and the money invested by First Baptist Church to renovate it, the vision is being realized. This 30-year-old dilapidated shell of a building has become the Jo Ann Carter Harrelson Center, home to Phoenix Employment Ministry, a non-profit organization that helps its needy clients find meaningful, productive employment. It's also home to Life Transitions, an organization that helps ex-offenders find homes and jobs as they transition back into society, and Life Builders, an adult Bible study organization. It's the temporary home of the Community Arts Center as its building undergoes renovation, and soon

it will become the home of WIRE, the Wilmington youth center for Inspiration, Recreation, and Education, a project from Communities in Schools to serve at-risk upper middle and high school students by giving them the tools they need to succeed and help them stay in school.

We should thank the people from First Baptist Church, and the individuals who serve on the board of the Harrelson Center, for their vision. They're turning this building from a place of incarceration to a place of transformation. We need more far-sighted people with vision and fewer near-sighted ones.

That's what we think.

• Is your congregation near-sighted or far-sighted?
• What long-term vision is simmering in your congregation?
• What keeps that vision from coming to the front burner?
• How do you share the far-sighted vision with the near-sighted critics?

Sacrifice and Delight

Ministry is a privilege.

Finally, I want to say a word about leadership, or, more precisely, the "art" of leadership. Because I see leadership as art, there are not a lot of rigid rules I can offer to govern how to do it. Good leadership is accomplished more by "feel" than it can ever be by "constitution and by-laws."

Now there is some measure of presumption when one offers such words about leadership, but it is what we as church leaders are expected to do—lead. While the First Baptist Wilmington staff has not perfected the art, we have sought to practice it with some degree of intentionality.

Scott Peck, in his most disturbing book, *People of the Lie*, observed that it is "much easier to be a follower than a leader."[1] We all knew that. He went on to say that when you follow, "There is no need to agonize over complex decisions, or to plan ahead, exercise initiative, risk unpopularity, or exert much courage." He was right.

All of that is to say that if you are going to lead, you had best want to lead and to be willing to pay the price of leadership, which, at times, can be quite high. You simply must not be afraid to lead. That was a lesson I had to learn.

Hang around a church long enough and you will hear ministers complain about the "burden of ministry." But to do so is to begin from a negative point of view. It will always lead to misery.

A more helpful view of ministry was painted for me by Alan Jones, long-time dean of Grace Cathedral (Episcopal) in San Francisco, who spoke of ministry in terms of "sacrifice and delight." Ministry is both of these, but it is not a burden. And while there may be some sense of sacrifice in doing ministry, it is completely overwhelmed by the delight, whether we are laity or clergy.

We must remember the God whom we serve and the high calling that has been laid upon each of us. As Reggie McNeal reminds us: "Leaders operating from a sense of mission care about not only what they do but how they do it. They pursue excellence, not for its own sake but for the sake of the mission that orders their lives. Pursuing excellence with this motive is not a burden; it is a privilege."[2]

Indeed, a life of ministry in the church is a privilege. We simply must approach it for what it is with the best we have to offer. It has been the confessed aim of each member of our staff to model excellence in whatever we seek to do in the name of Jesus Christ. We just need to remember that it can be quite messy along the way, especially when we seek to exercise leadership, because leading people involves taking them to a place they might not have otherwise gone or to a place they cannot go by themselves.

As a leader, it is important to create an atmosphere where church members and staff feel the freedom to try new things without fear. We need to celebrate those efforts in worship. People need that kind of encouragement. The pulpit is the place to call people to a new and faithful way of being the church and to help them imagine something different than their current reality.

The pulpit is also the one place where you get to paint a picture of the future—not necessarily a grand plan, but a better way. Most sermons lend themselves to the telling of a story. When those stories come out of your church and involve your people, they take on a power all their own. We saw it all the time. In almost every story like that, you will often find the elegant collision of hope and imagination.

Seth Godin, in his little book, *Tribes*, observed: "The secret of leadership is simple: Do what you believe in. Paint a picture of the future. Go there. People will follow."[3]

While we did not consciously follow this formula in my twenty-five years at FBC Wilmington, in retrospect, this path seems to best capture how we did the things we did. Of course, the most important piece of the journey is to "do what you believe in." Continually prompted by the Holy Spirit, this is what we sought to do.

After hearing author Brian McLaren speak at a CBF General Assembly in Charlotte several years ago, I approached him after the session to ask a question. He had spoken about how the landscape of American Christianity and culture had changed and the responses that would be needed for the church to engage all of this change. I told him about our church with ministers preaching in robes, with the big pipe organ and the very limited parking. I then told him that I felt led to guide the church into a new way of understanding its mission and ministry in our city. His response stunned me.

He said, "Mike, you have a done a good job at your church, but you need to forget about trying to lead change in a church like that. It is simply too much hard work. Go back home, enjoy your ministry, and know that they will always look back on your years as the golden years." I left that conference angry and with his words ringing in my ears.

Several years later, and after much of what has been written in this book had transpired, I attended another conference in Bethesda, Maryland, where McLaren was speaking. You see, I bore him no ill will and I really liked much of what he was writing those days. During a break, I bumped into McLaren in a hallway. I reminded him of our encounter after the Charlotte meeting. While he did not remember me, he did remember our conversation. "So, how are you doing?" he asked.

With some emotion in my voice, I told him that I had made the choice to not listen to his advice. I told him the good things that had taken place at FBC in those intervening years and of how we had grown and of how God had been with us on each step in the journey. I told him that he was right about one thing: The work had been hard. But I also told him how much fun it had been.

As he listened to my story, a big smile broke across his face, and he said, "I'm so glad you did not listen to my advice, and I am really glad you did listen to the Spirit's prompting." So am I.

One important caveat must be offered regarding our story at FBC. A lot of people have wanted to talk about the growth we experienced, more than doubling our attendance in an old downtown church with no off-street parking. Although that did happen and we were intentional about it, the numerical growth was simply a by-product of everything else that took place in the life of the church—and it took twenty-five years. There was no short cut.

Amazingly, most of the transformational events in our story took place in the last ten of those twenty-five years. Those are the experiences that people want to figure out how to replicate. But none of those events would have happened without the work of the first fifteen years. Everything in those early years was foundational for what happened in the last ten. It really was a long obedience in the same direction.

Our purpose in writing *Hopeful Imagination* has been to offer you encouragement. As you have listened to our story, we hope you were thinking about your story and about what God wants to do next in your life and in your ministry and in your church.

Listen for the whispers. Pay attention to the groans. Celebrate the praiseworthy. And in so doing, may you experience abundant "hope" in Jesus Christ, and may your "imagination" be fueled by the power of the Holy Spirit.

Notes

[1]M. Scott Peck, *People of the Lie* (New York: Simon and Schuster, 1983), 223.
[2]Reggie McNeal, *Practicing Greatness* (San Francisco: Jossey-Bass, 2006), 94.
[3]Seth Godin, *Tribes: We Need You to Lead Us* (New York: Portfolio, 2008), 108.

For help and encouragement as you engage your congregation in a journey of Hopeful Imagination, visit our website at www.HopefulImagination.com.